S0-ACA-210

DATE DUE

MAR 28 1963

AUG 8 1970

DISPOSITIONAL PROPERTIES

George Kimball Plochmann, GENERAL EDITOR

ADVISORY BOARD:

Irving M. Copi, *University of Michigan*

Wayne A. R. Leys, *Southern Illinois University*

Richard McKeon, *University of Chicago*

Newton P. Stallknecht, *Indiana University*

DAVID WEISSMAN

DISPOSITIONAL

PROPERTIES

FOREWORD BY

George Kimball Plochmann

SOUTHERN ILLINOIS UNIVERSITY PRESS
Carbondale and Edwardsville

Copyright © 1965 by Southern Illinois University Press

All rights reserved

Library of Congress Catalog Card Number 65-11655

Printed in the United States of America

DESIGNED BY ANDOR BRAUN

B
945
W3983
D5

To my family,

and in memory of my father

FOREWORD

THERE IS A CHARMING ESSAY by Samuel McChord Crothers which tells of a young man who leaves with his teacher a manuscript, hoping it will be read. "It is,"calmly says the young man, "only the first chapter, in which I explain the Universe." Admirable as this sense of ultimacy and comprehensiveness may seem, our first response is that the student in question had overextended himself, and that Aristotle might have remarked that system-building, even more than political science, is not for the young.

On the other hand, Paul Weiss (in *Modes of Being*) has lamented that philosophy has, in the twentieth century, lost its feeling for system and wholeness; and with his notion that the characteristic form of philosophy is chiefly the grand architecture, I strongly agree. A philosophical labor — or any intellectual effort, for that matter — is uncompleted without a wholeness of the subject-matter upon which that labor is expended, and one feels more intensely the appropriate awe in the presence of a great sequence of ideas which, right or wrong, seek to account for the widest stretch of facts of which life and reflection have made us fully aware.

Now comes David Weissman with an entire book about one point, and while the modesty of this attempt would be considered becoming, someone accustomed to the impressive edifices of Kant, Hegel, or even Whitehead would be disinclined to give this new book its due credit, unless he could be convinced that the work does lead into a system of its own.

We can persuade this hesitant reader to see that it does in two ways, I think: by pointing out the centrality of its problem, and by giving limits of the implications of its solution — implications which are suggestive for the tackling of a host of related problems. That the original problem of dispositional predicates *is* important is scarcely to be denied. Mr. Weissman has chosen for his topic the ancient but now partly-buried notion of power or potentiality, and he has discussed this chiefly as its solution points to the human mind, having, for the sake of compactness, let other types of biological powers, together with inanimate powers, take second rank in many sections of his discourse. The consequences of solving this problem can be numerous; theories of knowledge, of learning, and of ethical choice will be instantly and crucially affected. Strong hints are supplied, moreover, for dealing in very specific ways with sub-mental dispositions, and even those of bodies with or without planned mechanical function.

The book is set in the form of four long arguments that converge upon a single point, like the four great roads to Rome. Bearing down from the north, the Via Flaminia is an intricate discussion of the shortcomings of David Hume's account of mind as ideas and impressions, and of these in turn as no more than bits and pieces. From the east, the Via Tiburtina consists of a briefer treatment of certain contemporary accounts, mainly those of Carnap and Braithwaite, a treatment designed to show that their discussions of the question in terms of sentences leads to denial of some inescapable facts about the character of time-sequences. From the west comes the Via Aurelia, and here the Wittgenstein of the *Philosophical Investigations* is under consideration. He has, according to Mr. Weissman, proposed a theory of the starkest behavioristic sort, and a chapter of considerable thoroughness is dedicated to showing that Wittgenstein's explanation, which is aimed at giving proper meanings to terms held to be appropriate to the subject-matter of learning and knowledge, has run into collision with circumstances of consciousness and coming to know and forgetting upon which all of us must agree. Then there is the Via Appia, leading from the ancient Greek world, and appropriately enough this is a presentation of Aristotle and his theory of acts and potencies in real things.

Not all roads lead to Rome, in this book; most of them stop short, somewhere out in the suburbs of truth. Only the noble Appian Way takes us into the city, and even Aristotle is thought to require certain modifications and corrections before his work can be made to suggest a wholly adequate solution to the problem. Although Aristotle, slightly modified, is made to supply hints for the major part of the solution, this book is not written by someone for whom Aristotle's definitions and demonstrations are definitively true, someone for whom non-aristotelian debate is nothing but shadow-boxing. There is no appeal here to a perennial philosophy, no citing of collateral authorities as if they — I mean such men as Thomas Aquinas and John of St. Thomas — had themselves made all of the alterations required to perfect the teachings of The Philosopher. Rather we are treated to an independent and secular account of Aristotle, which is, outside of biological science and poetic theory, somewhat unusual nowadays.

The question which this book raises — and answers to the satisfaction of at least one reader — is how to steer a course between a doctrine of the mind as no more than a series of acts, on the one hand, and a doctrine of mind as a kind of unitary object, what one might call a block of cognition, on the other. The solution is to show first of all that there must be potentiality in the universe, and then to show that the mind is shot through with this potentiality — that here if anywhere there must be a nice balance between events that do take place and events that can take place.

The problem Mr. Weissman has really set for himself is to achieve a full and satisfactory explanation of thinking as a process partly continuous, partly discrete. But before he can even reach the turn in the road where such a problem can be formulated, he must consider the more general question, do substances in general have possibilities and tendencies? Here, I think, his answer is emphatic; after tracing the ways in which matter behaves in very obvious instances — bodies falling, litmus paper changing color, trees growing, and so on, he concludes that any account which ignores the middle ground between pure not-being and pure being, and also denies the distinction between a wholly undifferentiated potentiality and a partly-determined one, is bound to come to grief.

There is the second, and to my mind even more interesting question, and though the author is a little briefer in his treatment, it really forms the crux of his argument. It relates as we pointed out a moment ago, to the continuity and discreteness of thinking. Interpreting the flow of thought as being without any break at all would lead to an account of mind in which opportunities for deviation under duress from chance, from external events, internal desires, or even from the logic of rational inquiry would vanish, with an encapsulated mentality the only thing left. On the other hand, overemphasis on the discontinuity of ideas, their discreteness one from other, leads not only to a wrong conception of their substrate, a supine, passive mind, but also to a confusion regarding the very nature of the ideas as well. Thus if we take ideas as flitting, fragmentary, and "perpetually perishing," we must resign ourselves to an account allowing for no dialectical interconnections of them, or dialectical transformations either. Moving backward from such ideas, we are led to the doctrine of mind as a collocation, a faggot, with no real inside or outside. Moreover, the consequences for the interpretation of behavior are serious; there is now little or no way to attach a man's inner consciousness to his overt actions, either one-to-one or in constellations.

In the course of his study of thinkers representative of viewpoints he opposes, Mr. Weissman pauses from time to time to find solid principles for his own alternative. As a good dialectician, he discovers these principles by making only the slightest possible alterations in the materials supplied by those whom he has taken on as opponents, and this he has carried through, I think, only after he has done the best possible in trying to elicit truth from, and demonstrate falsity in, their pronouncements.

The methodological approach that Mr. Weissman employs varies with the character of the philosophies he is expounding or refuting; thus he moves quickly into a discussion of predicates when Austin, Carnap, or Braithwaite are before him, but adopts a psychological ground in assessing Hume and Wittgenstein. The final answer to his problem, however, is in terms of neither of those, but is a cautious appeal to the metaphysics of being, for which he makes use of Aristotle. But regardless of this shifting attack, what he is trying to do is to establish that bodies and minds must have *insides* — and that accordingly the way we talk about them must allow for predicates indicating capabilities, dispositions, tendencies. One might well imagine an assault by Henri Bergson upon Herbert Spencer for the latter's willingness to take the forms of life as inert bodies content merely to adjust to external conditions, unable to hold, let alone exhibit, any capacities in advance of what they actually do. The breath of life, for Spencer, is not the breathing but the breathed — and that which is breathed is chiefly imposed from outside, by alien, coincidental forces. Professor Weissman has little use for such inertness, whether it be taken as an image of matter itself or of the mind — he feels that if he can establish real potentiality in matter it will not be hard to show it in the mind too — and in the course of his study takes pains to show that all the phenomena concomitant to the nature of mind itself, such as attention, learning, following rules, causal associations, and so on, are incomprehensible when dispositions or potentialities are thrown out of court.

Mr. Weissman has expounded his doctrine, both on its negative and positive side, with a searching attentiveness to detail and to the possibilities for objections that his oponents might raise. His lettered and numbered outlines will provide help to the reader who wishes to thread his way carefully through the text. I am confident that anyone who has sampled no more than the first few pages will very quickly become a reader of that kind.

As a member in the Philosophical Explorations Series, this book fits well. It attacks old assumptions both vigorously and painstakingly, and although the work scarcely elaborates a positive doctrine of the mind and all that it does or can do, nevertheless Mr. Weissman clears a new and likely path in what has in recent decades become a thicket of hasty assumptions, partial arguments, and consequent wrangling disputes.

George Kimball Plochmann

Southern Illinois University
February 21, 1964

ACKNOWLEDGMENTS

THIS BOOK was started and largely finished when I was the student of Professor J. N. Findlay at King's College, the University of London. It was Professor Findlay who first suggested that I should provide an analysis of dispositional properties, and it was he who encouraged me when my ideas began to deviate from the fashionable views on this subject. I hope that the finished manuscript shows the degree to which I have profited from having had a teacher who respects the integrity of his students even while he tries to make constructive but critical philosophers of them. Professor Findlay has recently published an article titled "Metaphysics and Affinity" (*The Monist*, Vol. XLVII, No. 2, [Winter 1963]) where he outlines the principles of a naturalistic metaphysics and theory of knowledge. I intend that this book should be an example of the sort of analysis which he proposes.

In its final statement, my work reflects the influence of numerous conversations with Professor David Rynin. Professor Rynin has helped me to sharpen my understanding of a variety of points, but I am especially grateful to him for having forced me to defend my belief that dispositions should be analyzed in terms of real potentiality, and not by reference to causal laws.

Professor George Kimball Plochmann has several times

had to convince me that earlier drafts of the book were not so good as I had thought they were. He was right in every case, and I am indebted to Professor Plochmann for the care which he has taken in editing the manuscript.

William Mallory was kind enough to read an early draft of the book, and many of his suggestions have been incorporated into this final version.

There are several people who have helped to sustain me in a variety of nonacademic ways. I hope that they will accept this book with my deepest gratitude.

David Weissman

Trespiano, Florence, Italy
February 15, 1964

CONTENTS

PHILOSOPHICAL EXPLORATIONS

INTRODUCTION

Contemporary empiricists frequently express their antimetaphysical bias in the style of ordinary language analysis. They
say that metaphysical problems may exist, but that we have
no reason to believe that they do until it is established that
metaphysical issues have not been generated by misinterpret-
ing various rules of linguistic usage. Philosophers who talk in
this way are as confident as empiricists have traditionally been
that metaphysics has no subject matter and no method, but
nonetheless they dare invite us to prove that there are legitimate metaphysical issues, and they even specify the circumstances in which they would admit that metaphysical problems do exist. Their attitude is almost conciliatory when we
compare it to the antimetaphysical strictures of a generation
ago, and I think that this fact should encourage those of us
who are metaphysicians to prove that our analyses meet the
empiricists' requirements. This suggestion is not prompted
by an ecumenical spirit. Analyses which prove that metaphysical problems are sanctioned by ordinary language will at
very least succeed in demonstrating that the statement of
these problems is meaningful. Empiricists may subsequently
reject the arguments and definitions by which we try to solve
these problems, but this will require counter-arguments. Extravagant claims of meaninglessness will no longer count as
answers to a metaphysician's claims.

It is with this in mind that I propose to accept the empiricists' challenge. I shall argue in this introduction that, first, there is a rule of linguistic usage which commits us to the view that minds and objects have *dispositional properties*, and that, second, there is no way of interpreting this rule which will justify the refusal to give a philosophic, but non-linguistic, analysis of these properties.

John Austin supports both of these conclusions in a paper where he discusses two opposing claims which contemporary philosophers have made about "can"- and "could have"-sentences.[1] Austin writes:

> There are two quite distinct and incompatible views that may be put forward concerning "ifs" and "cans," which are fatally easy to confuse with each other. One view is that wherever we have "can" or "could have" as our main verb, an "if"-clause must always be understood or supplied, if it is not actually present, in order to complete the sense of the sentence. The other view is that the meaning of "can" or "could have" can be more clearly reproduced by *some other verb* (notably "shall" or "should have") with an "if"-clause appended to it. The first view is that an "if" is required to *complete* a "can" sentence: the second view is that an "if" is required in the *analysis* of a "can"-sentence.[2]

The first of these claims is partly correct, though as we shall see, it is not completely so; it is true that an "if"-clause is *sometimes* required to complete the sense of a "can"- or "could have"-sentence. Thus, we can imagine that a company director is remarking to an opponent on the board that he could have ruined the man at the day's board meeting, although he did not. The director would be describing what he might have done if he had controlled one more vote, and his complete statement would read: "I could have ruined you this morning, if I had had one more vote." For want of satisfaction of the condition described in the if-clause, the director was not in a position to replace the opponent with an ally, but if the condition had been fulfilled, he would have been able to do so. Generally, "can"- and "could have"-sentences which require completion by an if-clause may be translated by "will be in a position to act if" and "would have been in a position to act if," and in both cases, the if-clause states a necessary condition for being in the position. Had the condition been fulfilled in our example, the director would have had the capacity and the opportunity to act, and his desire to ruin an opponent would have been sufficient then to have assured the man's defeat.

While recognizing that this first account has some basis in linguistic usage, Austin denies that we must always complete "can"- and "could have"-sentences with an if-clause. His reasons are these:

> It is easy to see why it may be tempting to allege that it always requires an "if"-clause with it. For it is natural to construe "could have" as a past subjunctive or "conditional," which is practically as much as to say that it needs a conditional clause with it. And of course it is quite true that "could have" may be, and very often is, a past conditional: but is is also true that "could have" may be and often is the past (definite) indicative of the verb "can." . . . Exactly similar is the double role of "could," which is sometimes a conditional meaning "should be able to," but also sometimes a past indicative (indefinite) meaning "was able to": no one can doubt this if he considers such contrasted examples as "I could do it 20 years ago" and "I could do it if I had a thingummy."[3]

This is to say that there are occasions when "can" and "could have" are used in indicative sentences which report that someone or something has or had the capacity to perform in a certain manner.

Together with statements having dispositional predicates such as "fragile," "is weak," and "is red," these indicative "can"- and "could have"-sentences are the traditional focus of dispute when philosophers argue for and against the reality of dispositional properties. Where properties are conceived as the qualities, aspects or states [4] of any distinguishable thing, be it a mind, object, number, relation or event, the issue is to determine whether dispositional properties should be numbered among the states (understood as present and enduring conditions) of substances. Dispositional states have frequently been described as the properties which qualify substances for the suffering or initiating of effects, and hence, they are also known as causal or productive qualities and as powers.

If we suppose that indicative "can"- and "could have" sentences do in fact report that things have and have had real dispositions, we will imply that a sensitivity, for example, is as genuine a property as shape, and we will be responsible for giving an account, called a *realist* theory, of the categorical features of dispositional properties. This account would be an analysis of the manner in which dispositions function as causal properties, and in addition to and by way of the discussion of what they do, it would be an analysis of what dispositions are.

Enthusiasm for this project will be shown in varying degrees, and empiricists especially will regard it with undisguised abhorrence. They are certain to demand that every realist theory be subject to the principle that statements about the world are meaningful, only if we can imagine the difference which their truth or falsity would make to our perceptions. This is the verifiability principle, and empiricists who designed it supposed that they could put an end to all metaphysical theorizing by stipulating that observability be made the test of meaning and truth. Verificationists will have no doubt that a realist theory of dispositions cannot satisfy their principle, and that consequently the theory has no place in rigorous philosophic thinking.

A man who affirms the reality of dispositional properties will admit that the properties are unobservable, but though he goes on to insist that we can establish the reality of these properties by way of rational inference, his arguments are unlikely to convince the verificationists. Believing that perception is the only legitimate source of knowledge about the world, they will fasten upon the realist's admission that dispositions cannot be perceived, and they will deny that realist theories of dispositions can be true, or even meaningful. Taking it for granted that Berkeley, Hume and Moliere have permanently dispatched this notion, they are likely to be surprised that anyone could care to revive it.

Disconcerted though he may now be, the realist has taken Austin seriously, and the verificationists are obliged to tell him how indicative "can"- and "could have"-sentences ought to be interpreted. It does appear that these sentences ascribe powers to things, and supposing that one of the sentences be true, what else are we to believe but that a thing possesses a real power? Is it not normally the case that true indicative sentences are reports of worldly states of affairs?

One of the benefits of recent ordinary language analysis is its success in responding to queries like this one, and verificationists rely upon the techniques of this mode of analysis when providing what they regard as a final and decisive answer to realist objections. The verificationists argue that a man who interprets true "can"- and "could have"-sentences as reports that substances have powers is misguided, through having a theory which wrongly assimilates all linguistic functions to those of naming and reporting matters of fact. The more satisfactory view is said to be that language has many functions, and that naming and reporting are no more fundamental than the others even though it is true that they are more prominent. We are inclined to believe that there is something unique about these two functions, because the *surface* grammar of our language, with its subject-predicate statement forms, makes it appear that the narrative use of language is standard. But as it happens, sentences which have one of the less familiar linguistic functions are often disguised as indicative, reportorial sentences. In these cases, analysis helps us to penetrate the surface grammar of the sentence, and we come to understand its *deeper* grammar — and its proper function.

Arguing in this way, contemporary empiricists believe that they can disarm their opponent realist metaphysicians by showing that true "can" and "could have" indicative sentences have some other function than the one of reporting that substances have strangely unobservable though enduring properties. Empiricists claim that these apparently indicative sentences are in fact merely disguised predictions. To say that a man can or could have acted in a certain way is to say that he will act or would have acted in this way if supplementary causal conditions are or had been assembled.

If we accept this example of linguistic analysis together with their remarks about verifiability, the empiricists will apparently have two considerable objections against realist theories of dispositional properties: application of the verifiability principle will have proved that realist theories are meaningless, and the linguistic analysis will have demonstrated that there was never an occasion for proposing a realist theory of powers. It seemed that Austin had justified us in wanting to provide a realist theory when he argued that there are indicative "can"- and "could have"-sentences reporting that things have powers, but if a study of their deeper grammar reveals that these sentences are not indicative, then the consideration which might have projected us into a realist theory will have been swept aside. There will be nothing more to attract us in a theory that is unnecessary as well as meaningless.

No one supposes that this is the end of the matter. Some theory of dispositional properties is required, and the verificationists have a *reductionist* one to propose. Their theory has a destructive part which evaluates the claims of realist theories, and concludes, as we have just seen that dispositions have no unique status in being; dispositions, it says, are not any kind of property qualifying minds and physical objects. On its constructive side, the theory tries to convince us that a complete theory of dispositions is already implicit in reductive analyses of realist claims. Empiricists argue that the theory of dispositional properties calls for nothing more than an amplification of their analysis of dispositional language, and particularly of the counterfactual conditionals by which we describe how things will act and react if supplementary causal conditions are fulfilled.

This verificationist theory is the one that Austin is thinking of when he mentions the second view that people have held about "ifs" and "cans." Empiricists argue that "can"- and "could have"-sentences are properly analyzed into "shall-if"- and "should have-if"-sentences. Austin makes his point about this sort of analysis by considering the example which Philip Nowell-Smith has used to illustrate the theory in his *Ethics*. Offering the sentence, "Smith could have read *Emma* last night."[5] as typical of those which require analysis, Nowell-Smith suggests this expanded version of it: "He would have read it if there had been a copy, if he had not been struck blind, etc., etc., and if he had wanted to read it more than he wanted to read anything else."[6] This is to say, as verificationists do, that indicative "can"- and "could have"-sentences are predictions that things will act appropriately if supplementary causal conditions are fulfilled. The assertion that a man has a disposition is thus said to be nothing other than a claim that a certain counterfactual statement about him is true.

In a reply that is no less conclusive for its brevity, Austin writes:

> But so far from this being what we mean by saying he could have read it, it actually implies that he could not have read it, for more than adequate reasons: it implies that he was blind at the time, and so on.[7]

Austin is alluding to the counterfactual character of the sentence which Nowell-Smith would substitute for the categorical one, and he is asking us to suppose that a "can"- or "could have"-sentence is replaceable, in every case, by a "shall-if"- or "should have-if"-sentence. This would be to say that having a disposition is *equivalent* to acting in a certain way when appropriate conditions are satisfied. Consider, however, those occasions when supplementary conditions are not fulfilled, those times, namely, when we utter counterfactual conditional statements. If having the disposition is equivalent to the complex event of acting in a particular way when these conditions are fulfilled, then we will not have the disposition at times when we do not act for want of satisfaction of the conditions. But we do customarily suppose that people continue to have abilities when they are not displaying them, and Austin is prepared to reject an analysis of "can"- and "could have"-sentences which fails to provide for this common-sense view of dispositional properties.[8]

Finding themselves in the embarrassing position of having to affirm that a man cannot read when he is not reading, empiricists may temporize by admitting that indicative "can"- and "could have"-sentences do report matters of fact, while still denying that these sentences do sometimes report that substances have powers. As they will tell us, there are various other matters of fact for them to report. Thus, some indicative "can"- and "could have"-sentences inform us that there is moral, legal, or logical warrant for performing in a certain manner, and we say, "You can take that exemption" meaning that tax law permits you to do so. At other times, we use "can"- and "could have"-sentences to report that someone has an opportunity or desire, as we say, "You can take that long-delayed vacation (now that your family are grown)," and, with gritted teeth, "He can do it (he wants it badly enough)." There are numerous examples like these, but empiricists cannot appeal to them in order to support their claim that indicative "can"- and "could have"-sentences are never ascriptions of capacities, because Austin has already established that, whatever else they may tell us, some of these sentences do report that people and things do have enduring abilities and powers.

Empiricists will resist this conclusion on the grounds that application of their verifiability principle has already established that it makes no sense to talk as if powers are real. However unsatisfactory it may be to analyze dispositional properties in terms of counterfactuals, they will argue that this is only the positive side of their analysis, and that the negative part remains beyond criticism. But quite the contrary is true. It is the application of the verifiability principle which leads empiricists to deny that powers endure or have any reality whatsoever, and it is because of having applied this principle that empiricists subsequently construct a theory of powers which holds that powers do not endure. For this reason, Austin's criticism of the constructive half of the empiricist view fixes the responsibility for the theory's error on its negative part. If we accept Austin's common-sense view of dispositions, we have to conclude that it is arbitrary and unacceptably rigorous to suppose that observability is the sole test of reality. Therefore, we have to reject this principle as the one which ought to govern inquiries into the nature of dispositional properties. As ordinary language and common sense would have us believe, it is and always has been meaningful to say that powers are real and that they endure even while the minds and objects having them are inactive.

The immediate consequence of our rejection of the verifiability principle is the reopening of the possibility that there can be a valid realist theory of dispositional properties. This possibility obliges us to name a principle which may be adequate to direct the formulation of that theory.

In the chapters to follow, I have tried to revive and develop the classic Aristotelian theory of powers, and the shape of my analysis has been determined by a principle which is borrowed from Kant.[9] In its most general form, this principle directs us to accept some aspect of experience as given, and to account for this aspect by isolating the categorical factors in thought or in being which are its necessary conditions. This principle is evidently more permissive than the verifiability principle, for empiricists deny the reality of everything which cannot be conceived as a possible object of perception, while the Kantian principle encourages us to admit the reality of every factor to which we must infer in accounting for the occurrence of that aspect of experience which we have accepted as given. This does not mean that conditioning categorical factors are real in the way that entities such as minds and chairs are real, but it does require us to provide for these factors, when, as part of our analysis of substance, we total up the categorical distinctions which prevail in thought and nature.

As I have so far outlined it, the application of this principle may seem to be identical with the empirical method of tracing antecedent causal conditions when we have noticed their effect; but though there are similarities in these two methods, there are also two, fundamental differences. First, Kant's principle focuses our attention upon *categorical* factors which *logically* condition that feature of experience which we have accepted as given; we are not interested in particular efficient causes. This is the difference between explaining the fact that events have causes by referring to the reality of causal laws, and the very different problem of determining whether it was the wind or a baseball that shattered the kitchen window. There are numerous examples of these logically conditioning categorical factors: the facts that there are no properties unless there are substances, no events unless there are causes, and no moral action unless there are moral principles are but a few of them. In each of these cases the particular claim being made may be disputed, but each of them can still be accepted as an example of what is meant by a logically conditioning categorical factor.

Acknowledging the reality of these logically conditioning factors, our next problem is to develop a method which will enable us to isolate the relevant factors in particular cases. This problem of method is the basis for the second difference between the application of the Kantian principle and the characteristics of scientific procedure. Metaphysics and science both require that inferences be drawn, but in the later case, our reasoning depends upon assumptions which are empirical generalizations, and consequently upon inferences which may be falsified, for the reason that these generalizations may not have the universal applicability credited to them. It will not do to say, on the assumption that broken windows are always shattered by the wind, that this *must* have been the cause in some particular case. Remembering baseballs and glass-fatigue, we know it would be rash to assert this.

Matters are different in the case of inferences which establish the reality of logically conditioning categorical factors. One premise to these arguments does make an empirical reference, but this premise is not an inductive generalization purporting to have universal scope, and there is no chance that an empirical discovery may falsify the inferences drawn from it. Rational arguments of the sort I have in mind develop as we attend to some feature of experience, and try to isolate the categorical distinctions relevant to its occurrence. We see a window fractured, and adopting the assertion describing this event and its cause as our first premise, we hypothesize that a particular categorical factor is a condition for the production of this effect by its cause. The idea of this categorical factor is a rational notion, and the remainder of the argument will be dedicated to refining this notion and to testing the claim that its object must be a factor in the world in order for the event of our example to occur as it indisputably has. Our procedure will require the application of one or a series of arguments having the form of the *reductio ad absurdum*. Thus, having decided upon a factor that may be a logical condition for the matter in question, we now deny that it is in order to work out the consequences of this assumption. Our denial is the second premise to the argument. If its entailments are in harmony with the assertion that events have occurred as stated in our first premise, it will follow that our initially positive claim about the relevance of this factor was mistaken. Our original conception will have to be successively modified until a final *reductio* shows that a proposition denying the presence of this factor entails that the event accepted as given should not have occurred. We can then affirm that this factor is a logical condition for the occurrence of the event. Notice here that we shall have done more than prove a claim about this example alone. We have been drawn to this event because it exemplifies the relationship of cause and effect, and not because of specific characteristics such as wind velocity and the shape of the splinters. Our argument will have provided a partial analysis of one categorical factor relevant to any causal relationship. Moreover, our claim about these relationships will have a *priori* validity for it will follow from a premise which cannot be denied because it makes an indisputable claim about experience as given, and from the principle holding that we cannot accept this premise and also another that contradicts it.

In adopting Kant's principle for the analysis of dispositional properties, I have accepted the fact that events have causes as the empirically given, and as the point of departure for inferences which are to determine the categorical factors conditioning this kind of change. The remainder of this book is largely given over to a justification of the claim that the reality of dispositional properties is one logical condition for the fact that interacting substances produce effects. The organization of the book does not always reflect the application of its governing principle, because I have sometimes deviated in order to take up various historical considerations and competing theories. Nevertheless, particular arguments will show that this principle has been steadily applied.

There are five chapters to the book, with the fourth chapter intended as the capstone of my argument. It is an attempt to specify the essential characteristics of dispositional properties. I have described them as the real potentialities qualifying the minds and objects which have them for participation in causal relationships. Real potentialities are said to have four characteristics: First, they condition the production of effects; in their absence, no effects are produced when substances interact. Second, potentiality is irreducible to actuality; potentiality is not identical with one or a series of present or possible observables. Third, potentialities are specific; the potentiality that enables a thing to burn is different from the potentiality for adding figures or being audacious. Fourth, potentialities are not free-floating; they are the properties of minds and bodies; while potentialities are irreducible to properties like the shape of bodies, they owe both their being as potentialities and their specific character to the being and character of the properties which mark the actuality of minds and bodies.

Two considerations in this account of dispositional properties have required prior development and justification. One of these results from my having described dispositional properties as conditions for the production of effects. On account of this, I have had to provide a theory of cause and effect relations which will require us to acknowledge the reality of potentialities. The analysis of causal connection, and

the causal relationship, appears in Chapter 1. I have argued
that an effect will necessarily occur if the proper set of causal
conditions is assembled. Potentialities will now be required in
order to explain why some things rather than others qualify as
members of the set of causal conditions.

The second consideration requiring special support is
the attempt to correlate dispositional properties with the
properties which, I have said, constitute the actuality of
things, and to argue that the former depend for their being
and character upon the being and character of the latter. This
argument is more easily made in talking of physical objects
than in talking of minds. Objects have properties such as
shape which are taken for granted by all of us, but it is not
evident that there are comparable properties marking the
actuality of minds. There is consciousness and its modifications, but consciousness is as indeterminate as prime matter,
and its modifications are evanescent. I have required a factor
which is both as specific and as relatively enduring as are properties of physical objects. I believe that I have satisfied both
of these requirements by grounding mental potentialities in
the actuality of nonintrospectable mental states. Being sym-
pathetic to the thesis that minds and body are identical, I
would suppose that these mental states will sometime be regarded as the properties of cells in the brain, but this prej-
udice of mine has had no part in the arguments which I have
used to justify the claim that there are nonintrospectable
mental states.

I have chosen to argue for the existence of these states
by criticizing, in Chapter 3, a theory which assures us that we
have a complete account of mental activity in the description
of rules of behavior, linguistic as well as physical, which are
learned in order that people may respond appropriately to
publicly observable circumstances. Any number of behaviorists argue in this way, denying that nonintrospectable mental
states are necessary for mental activity. Discussion of any one
of these theorists would have served my purpose. I have preferred, however, to make a case for nonintrospectable mental
states by detailing and criticising the later-Wittgenstein's ob-

jections to this notion. Nearly every Wittgensteinian will see a grotesque misrepresentation in the attempt to identify Wittgenstein as a behaviorist, and for this reason, I have occupied a number of pages trying to prove that he is a behaviorist, and is therefore a reasonable opponent with whom to argue about the importance of nonintrospectable mental states for mental activity.

Of the remaining portions, Chapter 2 evaluates several contemporary, linguistic attempts to provide a satisfactory reductionist substitute for the realist analysis of dispositions. These are verificationist-inspired theories of the kind that were mentioned above and found wanting. The analysis of Chapter 2 takes up from where the above discussion ended, and it considers the "shall-if"-analysis of dispositional properties in some detail. The Epilogue is a series of replies to objections which may come to mind in reading the less polemical, more constructive parts of the book.

Readers will notice that I have made no special attempt to distinguish among dispositional properties, abilities, skills, habits, facilities, tendencies, capacities and powers. There are surely important differences among some of these properties. Skills, for example, are usually acquired, while habits and tendencies are often instinctual: habits are sometimes thought to be undirectional and blind, while a man with a rational capacity is able to perform in different ways and at will. I recognize these differences, but apart from a small section of the analysis in Chapter 4, I give no further attention to them. I have assumed that properties of these various types have a common nature, and that the features which may distinguish them are not so important as the ones they share. The analysis is devoted to an explication of that common nature.

HUME:

HIS REALIST SYMPATHIES AND
REDUCTIONIST CONVICTIONS

David Hume's philosophy is sometimes an arena for the competing realist and reductionist theories of dispositional properties. He alternately supports the principal elements of both views.

In the first portion of this chapter, I shall summarize the details of that section of A Treatise of Human Nature where Hume gives the details of his theory of abstract ideas and endorses the realist theory of powers. Hume believes that talk about abstract ideas is simplified talk about the fact that men think with determinate ideas which represent other ideas that can be brought to conscious reflection. "Can" in this instance is thought to mean that human beings have real powers for bringing the represented ideas to thought. The first section of my chapter is thus primarily a review of the difficulties which forced Hume to ground his theory of abstract ideas in a realist theory of powers.

The effect of the discussion is to sharpen our understanding of what is important to a realist theory, and to prepare for the second section of the chapter, where a five- and ultimately, a four-factor account of dispositions is laid down. I make no claim that Hume is an historical witness to the realist theory as I shall develop it in this second section. Hume's discussion of powers is suggestive, but there are no arguments in Hume to convince us that powers are real. The arguments which I shall propose sometimes begin with a reference to what Hume has said, but they never depend upon his authority for their truth. Moreover, though Hume's discussion of abstract ideas taken very literally could only justify the claim that a realist theory covers mental dispositions, I intend that it should also cover the dispositions of physical objects.

The last portion of this chapter takes up the skeptical criticisms which Hume sometimes directs at the idea of real powers. I shall argue that these criticisms are mistaken, and that we can prove this by showing how they entail unacceptable consequences.

Ia. *Hume's own account:* 1] *His realist theory of powers;* (a) *Abstract ideas are determinate ideas representing other ideas;* (b) *Ideas represented in thought by another idea are held in power.*

Hume sets the problem of abstract ideas in this way:

> A very material question has been started concerning *abstract* or *general ideas, whether they be general or particular in the mind's conception of them.* A great philosopher has disputed the received opinion in this particular, and has asserted, that all general ideas are nothing but particular ones annexed to a certain term, which gives them a more extensive signification, and makes them recall upon occasion other individuals, which are similar to them. As I look upon this to be one of the greatest and most valuable discoveries that has been made of late years in the republic of letters, I shall here endeavour to confirm it by some arguments, which I hope will put it beyond all doubt and controversy.[1]

This is Berkeley's suggestion, and Hume is elated by it, because Berkeley affords him an easy solution to a considerable problem.

The problem has its origins in Hume's dogmatic assertion that impressions are precisely determinate in their
quantity and quality, and that ideas are exact copies of impressions.[2] These suppositions could make it difficult for
Hume to explain the fluency of our thought. Imagine, for
example, that a claim is made about triangles in general. In
order to determine whether or not this claim is true, it should
be necessary for us to run through a series of ideas having
triangles of different shapes and sizes for their objects. But
this could be tedious and encumbering. The procedure would
be much simpler if there were a generic idea of triangularity
for us to examine. (I am assuming, as Hume does, that
geometric proofs are synthetic and depend upon imagined
constructions, that our ideas are discrete images, and that
thought is a stringing together of a series of images.)

Though he is aware of the conveniences that generic
ideas would afford, Hume wastes no time mourning for ideas
which he thinks we do not have. There would be no point in
this for he believes that thought is in no way disabled because
of having ideas which are determinate in every respect.
Berkeley has shown that this is a completely satisfactory state
of affairs by describing the associationist mechanism which
guarantees that thought will face any problem with the required subtlety and flexibility. Supporting Berkeley, Hume
writes:

> Tho' the capacity of the mind be not infinite, yet we
> can at once form a notion of all possible degrees of
> quantity and quality, in such a manner at least, as, how-
> ever imperfect may serve all the purposes of reflexion
> and conversation.[3]

Hume's only immediate problem is to show that mind
is equipped to think of determinate ideas as readily as he in-
sists that it can. His suggestion is that concepts are "customs"
or "powers."[4] Each of them is said to be a preparedness for
thinking of certain determinate ideas which have a resemblance or some other relation to one another. A single, and of
course determinate, idea is said to represent a concept in
thought, and reflection upon this idea is believed to be suf-

ficient to cue the power to release as many more determinate ideas to consciousness as are required by a particular intellectual need.

This solution is neat, but problematic. Hume, himself, is dubious about what we can know of the powers which are the heart of his theory of abstract ideas. He describes them as ". . . a kind of magical faculty in the soul which . . . is inexplicable by the utmost efforts of human understanding."[5] In the later pages of the *Treatise of Human Nature*, where Hume's skepticism is much more in evidence, the mystery of their operation will be an adequate reason for denying that powers are real. There is a discrepancy, however, between those sections and this early one. Far from taking this opportunity to deny that there are powers, Hume argues that we can only account for the generality of thought by admitting that powers are real. As he puts it:

> We must certainly seek some new system on this head, and there plainly is none beside what I have propos'd. If ideas be particular in their nature, and at the same time finite in their number, 'tis only by custom they can become general in their representation, and contain an infinite number of other ideas under them.[6]

The reductionist strain in Hume is so powerful, and Hume has been praised so often for his skepticism, that we cannot help suspecting that this passage unintentionally overstates the case. We are inclined to ask whether the theory of abstract ideas is not just as successful as before when it dispenses with powers, and merely states, as did Berkeley, that a single determinate idea represents other ideas in thought. Like it or not, I think we must admit that Hume cannot say this.

Hume has two difficulties to resolve if he is to claim that a determinate idea represents other ideas. The first of these bears on the relation of the represented ideas to the idea representing them in thought. There is a difficulty here concerning the mode of being of the represented ideas. The second problem is to explain how represented ideas may be brought to conscious reflection. Both of these difficulties compel Hume to recognize that there are powers. He does not discuss either problem; still, I should like to suggest the course by which these two difficulties may have led Hume to admit that powers are real. The question of the being of the represented ideas will be considered first.

According to Hume's theory of abstract ideas, a single, determinate idea, an image or a word, represents other determinate ideas in thought. In this formulation, the term "represents" is ambiguous. It might be used here to mean "pictorially represents," for when Hume first raises the problem of abstract ideas, it is this sense of the term which draws his attention. His opening passage has read: "A very material question has been started concerning *abstract* or *general* ideas, *whether they be general or particular in the mind's conceiving of them.*" The question of whether representative ideas are general or particular is to be decided by way of reference to the manner in which we conceive of them; but conceiving a thing is the same, for Hume, as having an image of it, and therefore, if ideas representing other ideas are general in the mind's conceiving of them, they will represent those other ideas as composite or generic pictures represent the things they portray.

Hume considers this possibility only in order to reject it. The notion of composite or generic pictorial representation is interpreted as meaning either that an idea is general ". . . by representing at once all possible sizes and all possible qualities, or by representing no particular one at all."[7] Both alternatives are rejected, because both violate the principle that ideas are perfectly determinate in every detail of quantity and quality. Hume concludes that there are no ideas which could serve as general pictorial representations of other ideas.

It may be felt that Hume has been too cavalier, and that the notion of general pictorial representation does have value for his account of abstract ideas. The image of a right triangle, for example, might represent all ideas of right triangles, or perhaps all ideas of right triangles having certain dimensions, but clearly, this will not do. Hume requires of ideas representing other ideas that they represent a *range of* ideas whose objects may radically differ from the object of the representative idea. The idea of a right triangle will have to represent ideas of triangles both scalene and equilateral, as well as right triangles themselves. The notion of pictorial representation is too limited to satisfy the requirements of Hume's theory of abstract ideas.

Some other sense of "represent" is required if we are to adopt the view that a single determinate idea can represent other ideas. That second meaning is found in the notion of a sign: a particular idea can represent an indefinite number of other ideas when it is a sign that stands for them to someone. This is the sort of representation that is built into Hume's theory of abstract ideas.

Ia.   2] *Two considerations forcing Hume to accept the reality of powers;   (a) He must account for the being of represented ideas;   (b) He must tell how represented ideas are brought to conscious reflection;   i. Factors stimulating mind to think of represented ideas are causal conditions;   ii. Mind is capable of acting as a causal condition only by virtue of its having acquired a power;   iii. Powers are thus factors qualifying minds to be causal conditions.*

The first difficulty prompting Hume to endorse a realist view of powers begins to emerge. A sign replaces something, and represents it to someone; but if there is nothing to be represented, the idea or object which is being regarded as a sign will cease to be one, and the sign-relation will be dissolved for want of one of its relata. This is no problem when physical objects are represented by a sign, because they endure whether or not we follow up the sign and go looking for them. It is not so obvious, however, that ideas continue to have a kind of being when they are represented. The represented ideas are not being thought about; this is the advantage of having a single determinate idea to stand for them. Are they annihilated when they are no longer reflected upon? If so, there will be nothing to be represented. The single, determinate idea will no longer be a sign of anything, and Hume's theory of abstract ideas will be worthless. Some provision must be made for the being of ideas which are represented by a sign in thought.

One can imagine a number of fanciful theories to account for the mode of being possessed by these represented ideas. It might be said that God is thinking of them, or that they somehow lurk in the unconscious mind. These are two versions of the argument that ideas are independent, and already determinate, subsistent entities before they are reflected upon. It might be said that calling them to consciousness is a matter of bringing them from one mode of being, subsistence, to another mode, a kind of existence. Passing out of conscious thought they would fall back into mere subsistence. If we philosophize in keeping with the tradition that entities should not be multiplied beyond necessity, we are certain to be leery of this solution. It effortlessly postulates a realm of subsistent entities when we suspect that closer logical scrutiny will reveal a way of accounting for the same facts of experience with greater economy.

As it happens, there are two theories by which we can account for the being of represented ideas, both of them more frugal than the subsistence theory. One theory says that represented ideas may be the objects of mental intentions; the other supposes that the ideas are held in power. In order to have made the most of the first view, Hume would have had to propose an intentional theory of mind. He could then have talked of the complex act by which consciousness registers the identity of something presented to it, regards that something as being the source of, or standing in relation to, other possible presentations, and anticipates the appearance of some one or more of those presentations. Having the idea of an isosceles triangle, we look beyond it, according to this theory, to the ideas it represents. The represented ideas are not the direct objects of thought, as the sign is, and represented ideas have being only insofar as we are prepared for their appearance as direct objects of consciousness.

Whatever the value of this intentional account — and there appears to be much truth in it — this is not the explanation of the being of represented ideas which is implicit in Hume. It cannot be, because Hume offers a mechanical, associationist theory of mind rather than an intentional one.[8] There is no need on Hume's theory for conscious anticipation of ideas: the ideas appear automatically when they have been cued by reflection upon ideas or impressions with which they have been constantly or frequently conjoined. But now, having dispensed with the notion of conscious intention, Hume is unable to provide for the being of represented ideas in so economical a way as does the philosopher who adopts an intentional theory of mind. The intentional theory requires no added assumptions in order to account for the being of represented ideas; they are said to have being just to the extent that they are anticipated as objects of consciousness, but this involves no assumptions beyond those already made by this theory. Hume, however, is required to make a special assumption, because his description of the rules of association can tell us nothing about the prior status of ideas which suddenly appear on the heels of impressions or other ideas. It is to make up for this deficiency in his theory that Hume must suppose that ideas represented by a sign are held in power.

I do not mean to suggest that the need to make this assumption makes Hume's theory a more complicated, more clumsy, and therefore less acceptable theory than the intentional theory of mind. To the contrary, for though the intentional theory often provides a more complete description of our mental life, it fails to give as comprehensive an account of the being of ideas represented by signs as does Hume's theory with its recognition of powers. The intentional theory does not tell us about the being of ideas which are neither present objects of conscious thought nor are anticipated as likely objects of thought. But this is the status of most of our ideas most of the time, and Hume's theory provides for the being of these ideas when he holds that they are held in power. If the intentional theory is also to account for these

ideas, it too must agree that they have being to the extent
that the mind has powers for thinking of them.

Helpful though the assumption is, there is no denying
that Hume's reference to powers appears gratuitous. Telling
us nothing about the manner in which these powers have
their being, Hume might as well have said that represented
ideas are subsistent entities. Many people will suppose that
this is all that could be meant by a reference to powers, and
it is in order to prove to them that Hume's explanation is
not an artificial one that we must turn to the second difficulty
in the claim that a single, determinate idea represents other
ideas in thought. That is the problem of telling how represented ideas can be made to appear as objects of reflection.

Hume's solution to this problem is implicit in his
abstractionist theory of concept formation. He argues that
there is a feeling of novelty in our encounters with something
new, until finally, after several meetings, "The novelty wears
off; the passions subside; the hurry of the spirits is over; and
we survey the objects with greater tranquility. By degrees the
repetition produces a facility, which is another powerful principle of the human mind."[9]

Somehow, minds that undergo the conditioning which
Hume describes are prepared, ever after, to respond intelligently to circumstances that were originally novel and
opaque. It is undeniable that something happens to the mind
between the time of its first encounter with an alien thought
or object, and the time when mind is able to function intelligently in meetings with ideas or objects of these kinds.
Supposing that Plato was mistaken and that we do not have
highly specific innate ideas waiting for perception or dialectic
to bring them to light, I see no choice but to infer that cognition has become possible, when repeated exposures to an alien
something have made an enduring impression upon the mind.
I think it reasonable to suppose that the mind has acquired
what we may call a new *mental state*. True, this phrase is
most often used to refer to a conscious state of mind, but that
sense is not intended here. This acquired state is rather a
nonintrospectable mental condition.

Hume does not allude to the mental state in the passage that is quoted above, but reference to it is implied when he does say that the mind acquires a facility. Acquisition of the facility would seem to be a consequence of having the mental state: repeated encounters with an alien object or idea have an impact upon the mind, and this in turn apparently accounts for our having the facility. For "facility," we may read "power."

An understanding of how men acquire powers is of help in explaining how represented ideas become objects of conscious reflection. We are better able to see this if we rephrase the original question, asking now *why* the acquisition of a power enables the mind to respond intelligently to an object or an idea. The answer is apparently that the possession of the power is a condition for the transformation of the relationships in which a man confronts circumstances strange to him. This is clearest in the case of encounters with unrecognized physical objects. Prior to the acquisition of a power, man and object are related as mere conjuncts in space and time. When the man has a power, their relationship changes its character, as he begins to think and act appropriately with respect to the object. We may say that his thinking or acting is an *effect* of having encountered it. A mere space- and time-conjunction has become a causal relationship whose conditions are the man and the physical object.

Most important for our purposes, the man is now able to respond intelligently, because he has acquired a power. The power itself is not a causal condition, but the man's possession of it is a condition for his entering the causal relationship. Recalling the remarks of the Introduction about the difference between logical and causal conditions, we say now that the power is a logical condition for the production of a change. Moreover, the possession of a power is a necessary qualification for anything which would contribute to the production of an effect.

We can accommodate these results to Hume's discussion of abstract ideas. Imagine a person who is asked to solve a problem or answer a question. We can suppose that he is asked to name all the kinds of butterflies visiting his garden. We have the beginnings of a causal relationship here in the particular idea being reflected upon, and the circumstances prompting the mind to conceive of other and related ideas. But as it happens, this man has never devoted any thought to butterflies, and he has no idea of the names given to the various species he often sees; it is pointless to expect an answer from him, until he has had an opportunity to study his field guide to the local insects. When we subsequently repeat our question after he has made his inquiries, the set of causal conditions will be complete, and the names we request will come to the man as objects of reflection. We can regard them as the effects produced by a set of causal conditions.

This is the answer to the second difficulty which has compelled Hume to adopt a realist approach to the problem of mental dispositions. The problem has been to tell how ideas required by thought are brought to conscious reflection, and the solution is that ideas are produced for consciousness by sets of causal conditions. Minds qualify to be causal conditions by virtue of having certain powers.

The resolution of this second difficulty makes it easier for us to understand what was implied by saying that represented ideas have being by way of being held in power. I did not mean that represented ideas are subsistent entities that wait, fully-formed, for the call to appear as objects of reflection; nothing of this sort is required. Represented ideas do have being, but they have it just to the extent that the mind is able to respond to the demands made upon it by thinking of the required ideas.

The likely objection to this will be that represented ideas obviously have no being whatsoever, if this is all that can be claimed for them. I think this is a little too strong. We can ascribe being to represented ideas in a way that we cannot ascribe it to ideas which cannot be thought, because there are no minds with powers for thinking them. In this way, all possible effects have being to the extent that there are things having the powers to produce them. This is a very pale and attenuated sense of "being," but it is enough to satisfy the requirements of Hume's theory of abstract ideas. A single determinate idea will be able to act as a sign representing other ideas, because this first idea, in conjunction with a mind having a power and a need of reflection, will be sufficient cause for bringing the required ideas to thought. Where the sign representing them is qualified to assist in their creation, the being of the represented ideas is satisfactorily guaranteed.

We may conclude that powers have been required to account for both the being of represented ideas, and for the mechanics of their appearance in thought. Powers — as we set out to prove — are indispensable to Hume's theory of abstract ideas.

Ib.   Correction of Hume's theory;   1] Analysis of reality of powers begins with recognition that causes produce effects; we must argue regressively from this;   2] Five factors to be provided for in generalizing from discussion of Hume: (a) Mind or object having a power;   (b) Effect this helps produce; (c) Supplementary causal conditions;   (d) Causal relationship of three foregoing together.

On the basis of information that we have gleaned from the analysis of abstract ideas, I propose to construct a realist theory of dispositional properties. This will not be an original theory; its outlines are perfectly explicit in Aristotle and in Leibniz, and as I have tried to indicate above, they are clearly suggested in Hume. Whatever is new in the theory is a result of my having to provide arguments in support of controversial claims which the theory makes.

Most contemporary philosophic attempts at theory-building are analyses of some variety of linguistic usage. Since Austin has already demonstrated that dispositional language is a promising field of analysis, it would be reasonable to suppose that a theory of real powers should also be the product of a linguistic analysis. Unfortunately, there is a fatal disability to this approach. Until someone proves (as I believe no one can prove) that our natural ways of talking about the world *must always* be symptomatic of distinctions and categories which have reality in being, it will be mistaken to assume that any linguistic analysis is a source of information about the world. This is to say that no realist theory can justify its claims if it restricts itself to an analysis of language. If we care to be realists, the preoccupation with language and thought must give way to an examination of things as they are. In the case of dispositional properties, this means that no analysis of dispositional language can be a satisfactory substitute for the attempt to construct a definition of powers which will reflect their condition in being.

The problem for those of us who would foresake language for being is to find a subject for analysis. How *does* one go about looking at things in the world in a way that will make them fit subjects for philosophic inquiry? The answer, I suggest, is that we fasten upon some aspect of experience, regarding it as the consequence of conditions which are logically antecedent to it. The subsequent philosophic analysis is an attempt to isolate these logical conditions and to prove that the given feature of experience necessarily presupposes their reality.

The realist analysis of dispositional properties begins in just this way. We are impressed by the fact that minds and objects of different kinds combine in many ways to produce effects, and we ask for an accounting of the categorical factors which make it possible for these effects to occur and which determine that they should be so various.

The merit of our discussion of Hume's theory of abstract ideas is its success in showing how powers function as one logical condition for the production of effects. Hume has argued that a single determinate idea can be a sign representing other ideas if the mind has a power, and that a represented idea will replace the sign as an object of thought whenever the mind having a power is prompted by some need of reflection. The succession of ideas in thought is a kind of effect, and, as I described them, the sign, the mind having a power, and the need of reflection are causal conditions for its production.

Two things about this effect are explained by reference to powers. First of all, the mind's possession of a power has been a condition for the *occurrence* of the change; in the absence of the power there would have been no succession of ideas in thought. Second, the *identity* of the power has been one of the factors which has determined the *identity* of the effect. The function of the power here is clearly independent of the fact that the character of the sign and the need of reflection also help to determine the identity of the effect. To establish this, we suppose that a saloonkeeper and a musician are given a free association test: as words are flashed on a screen, they record the ideas that come to mind. The sign and the need of reflection are constants now, and so we can only account for the test subjects' different responses to the word "bar" by supposing that the men have different powers.

There are five factors in this analysis of abstract ideas which are relevant to an account of the manner in which powers condition change. They are:

    I. The mind having a capacity;

    II. The change occurring in the mind that has the power;

    III. The supplementary causal conditions which consist of the sign in thought and the need of reflection, and which must be present if the change is to occur;

    IV. The causal relationship of these first three taken together;

    V. And the capacity, power or disposition of the mind.

Each of these factors is distinguishable from the others, because each of them has a special and indispensable function to serve in the complex event where causal conditions produce their effect.

If we take the passage of ideas through consciousness as our point of departure, any attempt to understand the conditioning powers will necessarily recognize all of these factors. Similarly, factors like these invariably emerge whenever any sort of change is taken as a point of reference for the analysis of dispositions. In the remaining pages of this section, I want to give a more careful and generalized description of each of the five factors. There is nothing problematic about the first three factors, but the last two, the causal relationship and the dispositional property, will require extended attention.

i. Minds and physical objects qualify to be causal conditions, because they have powers. Being properly disposed they may suffer a change, or initiate one in some other thing.

"Things have powers" is an expression which is no more illuminating for coming so easily to the tongue: "bodies have shape," we know what that means, but *how* do things have powers? This is a notion that cannot be clarified, I think, so long as we insist that shape and size are the paradigm examples of all properties. Moreover, there is little hope of understanding how things have powers, until we have determined what powers themselves are.

Nonetheless, some clarification of this idea is possible if we refer back to the discussion of abstract ideas. It was said that minds come to have facilities when repeated encounters with phenomena of the same kind have resulted in the acquisition of a new nonintrospectable mental state. It appears that having the power is conditional upon having acquired the mental state. Some mental states, of course, might be innate, and this would account for minds' having other powers. Drawing a parallel distinction in the case of physical objects, we can suppose that they have powers, because of having certain molecular structures, or because of their gross physical characteristics. I suggest, in anticipation of Chapter 4 where this will be worked out in detail, that the way in which things have powers is best, and so far as I can see, only, understood through an examination of the relation of powers to nonintrospectable mental states and the physical properties of objects.

ii. The product of a complete set of causal conditions is a change. For our purposes, change is to be conceived, in the broadest sense, as any difference in condition which is produced by or inflicted upon a mind or physical object. This may be a change in the direction of a man's present and on-going physical activity, a modification in the object or tone of his conscious awareness, a change in physical position or structure, and so on. The only changes that stand outside of this range are the ones which are consequences of the application of some normative principle. The enfranchisement of twenty-one-year-olds is an example of the kind of change which this discussion does not cover.

III. Possession of a power is not sufficient in itself to bring about the change to which a mind or object is disposed. There are always several other conditions whose nonfulfillment would prevent the occurrence of the change. Some things appear to be completely self-starting and free of external influence, but this is only a superficial conception of them. There are always background conditions at least as obvious as air pressure and gravity to be taken into consideration. These are examples of the supplementary conditions which must be satisfied if change is to occur.

Nelson Goodman has exposed the difficulties of stating a general logical rule which will help us to distinguish in any particular situation between nonrelevant factors and true supplementary causal conditions.[10] Goodman argues that suggested rules either fail to exclude all nonrelevant factors, or exclude all of these, and some of the supplementary causal conditions too. This does not mean (and Goodman does not say) that the assembly of supplementary causal conditions is not necessary for the production of a change. Much to the contrary, the very attempt to formulate this general rule presupposes that there is a difference between factors which have nothing to do with the occurrence of a change, and those conditions which help to produce it. Purely logical difficulties in stating the rule do not make this distinction any less clear.

IV. Let us suppose that a set of causal conditions is complete; the mind or object having a disposition and a number of supplementary causal conditions are all present and properly arranged with respect to one another: in the moment when the set is completed, an effect is produced; some one or several of the causal conditions is changed in some way. These are the two stages of a causal relationship; and I want to consider them in the order in which they occur.

Ib.   2] (d)   i. *First stage of causal relationship;*   ii. *Second stage of causal relationship;*   iii. *Answers to three objections: that causal relations are merely spatial and temporal, that so tenuous a bond will not always secure effect, and that it is only probable that effects will ocur;*   iv. *Reassertion of view that complete sets of causal conditions will always produce their effects;*   v. *Explication of* production *and* existential dependence.

There is justification for saying that the assembly of a set of causal conditions is fortuitous. Imagine that a man is prompted to think of his daughter by snatches of a stranger's conversation, or that a truck runs into his parked car. I think it could be said of either case that the causal conditions which we notice, and regard as accidentally conjoined are in fact the last phases of historical strands which have moved towards convergence; and certainly, this view could be supported without recourse to the notion of final cause. Convergence of the strands could be blind and unintentional, and determined by the piling up of efficient causes in the separate strands. All of this notwithstanding, however, the most resolute determinist is likely to agree that reference to these historically continuous strands does not eliminate chance from the assembly of a set of causal conditions. He would admit that the *origins* of the convergent strands are wholly independent of one another. At any time prior to their convergence, nonoccurrence or, later, annihilation of one strand would have had no effect on the contemporaneous history of the other strand. Their independence of one another is the consideration which makes it accidental when two historical strands do eventually collide.

This is just half of the causal relationship, however, and it is an entirely different matter when the set of causal conditions is complete, and the effect occurs. At this juncture, there appears to be no question of chance. Hume, for one, agrees that the change will *always* occur once the causal conditions have been satisfied. He writes at one point:

> For this is one of the most extraordinary circumstances in the present affair, that after the mind has produc'd an individual idea, upon which we reason, the attendant custom reviv'd by the general or abstract term, readily suggests any other individual, if by chance we form any reasoning that agrees not with it. . . . *If the mind suggest not always these ideas upon occasion, it proceeds from some imperfection of its faculties.*[11]

(Italics supplied.) Hume is saying: If required ideas fail to appear as objects of reflection, there must be something wrong with the faculties which normally provide these ideas for thought. In other words: If no ideas, then no (or at least imperfect) faculties. This is equivalent to: If faculties, then ideas. Hume would almost certainly agree that the absence of any of the relevant causal conditions, a need of reflection for example, would prevent the required ideas from appearing in thought, but whether or not I am correct in imputing this view to him, I suggest a substitution: instead of, "If faculties, then ideas," we now read, "If conditions, then ideas." When expanded, this will go: "When causal conditions are fulfilled, required ideas always appear as objects of conscious reflection."

The relation of cause and effect is defined, in reference to this passage, as the relation such that if (a and b), then c, and if not c, then not (a and b). This characterizes the relation of the causal conditions, e.g., a, the mind or physical object having a power, plus b, the supplementary causal conditions, and, their effect, c, the change that a and b jointly cause. The definition tells us that the assembly of a set of causal conditions is both sufficient and necessary for the effecting of a change. If we work from the currently popular view that causal relations are only conjunctions in space and time, these two ideas, causal sufficiency and causal necessity, will be understood in terms of the *regularity* or *frequency* with which the complete set of causal conditions and their effect are related. Thus, the notion of causal sufficiency will be taken to mean that the effect will occur whenever the set of causal conditions is complete. Causal necessity will be understood as the notion that occurrence of an effect is conditional upon the satisfaction of a set of causal conditions; the effect will occur when they have already occurred. Reasoning in these ways, it is possible to explicate the ideas of both causal sufficiency and causal necessity by merely giving two different emphases to the idea of regular conjunction in space and time; when causes occur effects will also occur, and effects occur whenever causes have already occurred.

I expect orthodox, reductionist Humeans to take exception to this account of causal sufficiency and necessity. It is true, they will say, that this analysis avoids the error of supposing that these are properties of a particular, occurrent causal relationship (Hume is thought to have exposed this error by reminding us that no one is able to *perceive* the sufficiency or necessity in a causal connection), but it is no less an error to reintroduce these notions by way of a definition which supposes that effects always occur when a complete set of causal conditions is assembled. There can be no justification for talking of sufficiency and necessity in these terms, because we cannot tell in advance that causal conditions will always produce their effect. Hume, if anyone, could be expected to know this, and his use of "always" must be dismissed as a careless slip.[12]

Reductionist Humeans do of course propose a frequency theory of causal relationships, but their account differs from the one I provided above in supposing that it is only very likely, rather than certain, that an effect will occur when a set of causal conditions is complete. The reductionists' version of the frequency theory holds that the same set of causal conditions normally succeeds in producing an effect, but it adds that the causal conditions may sometimes fail to produce that effect. No one of the complete set of causal conditions will be missing when the effect does not occur, and no extraneous factor will have intervened to prevent its occurrence; it will just happen that the normal set of causal conditions is present, and no change is produced.

This theory does allow for the possibility that the future may not always be like the past, but evident as that is, it may not be equally clear why this is a significant consideration. The reason, I think, is as follows: Both the effects-will-always-occur theory, and the theory that effects are only likely to occur, assume that cause-and-effect relations are merely relations of contiguity and succession. This assumption obligates both theories to distinguish genuine causal relationships from accidental conjunctions in space and time. A classic example of an accidental conjunction is that of a train which regularly departs from a station immediately after a blast from a nearby factory hooter. We establish that this is not a true causal relationship by turning off the hooter and watching the train pull away on schedule. Our experiment is a symptom of the fact that accidental conjuncts are independent and causally unrelated, and this fact in turn is the basis for the inference that accidental conjuncts are unlikely to be constantly conjoined.

This inference is valid for two kinds of accidental conjunction, and it can be stretched to cover a third: First, it is true of the majority of all instances of accidental conjunction; the instances in which things are only momentarily conjoined, as when cars pass on the road. Second, there are the examples of regular conjunction, like the hooter and train, where an experiment is required to prove that the factors are not causally related, and are unlikely to remain permanently conjoined. Third, there are instances where practical difficulties make an experiment impossible, as in the case of trying to prove that binary stars do not depend upon one another for continued existence, but where we can nevertheless imagine the sort of experiment that would prove the causal unrelatedness of the factors.

In contrast to all three of these classes of cases, constancy of conjunction is the typifying characteristic of the causal relationship; satisfaction of a set of causal conditions does result in the occurrence of a change, and nonoccurrence of the effect is evidence that the set of causal conditions has not been completed. Because of this difference, we accept regularity, or frequency, of conjunction as the test for identifying causal relationships. Both of the theories which we are considering are successful expressions of this criterion, because each of them fixes the standard for being a causal relationship at a degree of regularity which accidental conjunctions either cannot satisfy, or, as in cases like the binary stars, can be imagined not to satisfy.

This brings us back to the original problem: why, if both theories are equally satisfactory for identifying causal relationships, do we favor the theory that causes are only likely to produce effects, and reject the theory that the effects will always occur? The answer is that we favor the theory whose claims are most guarded. Here, the advantage belongs to the theory which conservatively admits that it is possible that causes and effects may not always be related. There would appear to be no reason to chance the more doubtful claim that mere conjuncts in space and time (which is all that causes and effects are supposed to be) will always be conjoined.

However much we are inclined to favor the theory that causes are only likely to produce their effects, it is undeniable that this theory is intellectually unsettling. If nature did break down, and no effect occurred when a set of causal conditions was assembled, we would be very hard-put to account for what had happened. It would do no good to explain the situation by arguing that one or more causal conditions had not been satisfied, or that an outside factor had inhibited production of the effect, because *ex hypothesi*, both inferences would be false. There would be just one possible line of inquiry: we could investigate the possibility that nature had experienced an upset that was limited in scope, but was so radical in its effect that the causal law once operative in situations like this was no longer operative. In the event that this was true, a set of causal conditions would never again, short of another radical upset, produce the effect with which they had been regularly conjoined in the past, and we would no longer have reason to be surprised that the effect had not presently occurred. This hypothesis could be easily tested. We could assemble the causal conditions another time, and watch for the result. If it happened, as is perfectly in harmony with the orthodox Humean theory, that the effect *did* occur when the test was run, it would be proof that the old causal law was still in force. Unless we were willing to suppose that an evil genius was toying with us, we would have to admit that our proposed explanation was mistaken. There would be no accounting now for the aberrant case where causal conditions were assembled and an effect normally produced by them did not occur.

This much is hardly the beginning. It would be obvious to us that the effect would have occurred if causal conditions had been sufficient to produce it; but it did not occur and so they must not have been sufficient. Looking back now at all those occasions when causes like these did produce effects, we would begin to wonder how they could possibly have done so. In each of those instances, the causes are presumed to have been exactly like these impotent ones before us; but, if the causes have not been sufficient now, how could they have been sufficient in the past? On the assumption that the causes were exactly like these, the answer must be that they were not sufficient. It should seem reasonable to us now that causal conditions of this kind should not produce effects, and we should find it completely inexplicable that, somehow, they did produce effects in the past.

When pressed to justify a theory which has these strange implications, its authors may tell us that this is one of those cases where there are no more reasons to be given: there is a real possibility that no effect may occur when causal conditions are assembled, but there is no telling how this failure could occur, or, in retrospect, how similar sets of causal conditions were able to succeed in producing effects. This reply is likely to remind us of the occasions upon which philosophers modestly decline to give explanations for ground-level differences in thought and nature. If asked, for example, to explain why there are so many kinds of primitive subatomic particles, we say that we do not know, and that short of God, no one else knows. Unfortunately, philosophers who propose the theory that we are considering have no recourse to this excuse, because they are not describing an ultimate, inexplicable difference in thought or nature. Orthodox Humeans have a theory that there are or might be disparities in being; a complete set of causal conditions normally produces its effect, but it need not do so, and sometime we may discover that the effect has not been produced when it should have been. This is not a statement of fact, but rather an *a priori* claim that the facts might be of a certain order. Philosophers who make this claim cannot avoid giving their reasons for making it; distinctions imputed to nature, rather than discovered there, do require justification.

Points made in behalf of the theory will have to satisfy two requirements: they must prove that distinctions made by the theory, and implications of those distinctions, are supported by argument; and they must show that there is a foundation in experience for the distinctions which are being used to give a logical description of causal relationships.

In the present case, there appears to be no possible rational justification for the distinctions that are drawn. No one can explain why a complete set of causal conditions may normally produce an effect, but sometime fail to do so when free of external interference; nor can anyone explain why effects should ever be produced if causal conditions are not always sufficient to produce them. As judged in terms of the first requirement, alone, the orthodox Humean theory is unsatisfactory.

Furthermore, this theory is not a proper characterization of experience. We never find that an effect sometimes occurs when all of a set of causal conditions are fulfilled, and sometimes does not. The men whose theory we are considering would answer this last charge by saying that they are taking a prospective view: so far the effect has always occurred when the proper set of causal conditions has been completed, but it is not necessary for it to do so in the future.

This cannot be an acceptable response. On the assumption of a frequency-theory of probability, it is hardly reasonable to assert that nonoccurrences of the effect, when causal conditions are fulfilled, are always saved for the future. To the contrary, nonoccurrences of the effect should be more or less evenly distributed in time. Philosophers who argue that it is only probable that effects will occur when causal conditions have been fulfilled, should recognize that their theory, taken in conjunction with a frequency-theory of probability, entails that there should be present-moment rather than future empirical evidence for the truth of the theory. It is a simple matter to test the theory on this count. Any number of activities in everyday life involve a causal relation, and are performed regularly. Under the circumstances, we should have substantial empirical evidence that effects need not occur when sets of causal conditions are complete. But as it turns out, there is no evidence; we are able to show invariably that nonoccurrence of an effect is owing to the absence of a causal condition, or to the intervention of an outside factor. This falsifies the theory that it is only probable that an effect will occur when a set of causal conditions is assembled, and it justifies our final rejection of the theory.

In view of its faults, I find it hard to see how anyone could hope to resuscitate this theory. Still, that does not mean that we are left with no theory about the relation between causal conditions and their effects. Much to the contrary: experience is our point of departure for the analysis of causality, and the regular conjunction of causes and effects in experience limits us to the inference that causes are either highly likely to produce effects, or will always produce them. When the first possibility is rejected, we are compelled to agree that causes will always produce their effects. Many philosophers will find this very hard to believe, and I admit that nothing which has been said up to the present about the effects-will-always-occur theory will have reassured them; so far, there have been no positive arguments to prove that the theory is true. This is the time to make up that deficiency.

Unusually, perhaps, for an argument intended to support a theory, I want to begin by proving that there is a fault in the principal assumption which I have been attributing to the effects-will-always-occur theory. The assumption I have in mind is the idea that the salient features of a causal relationship are exhaustively analyzed when we have described the spatial and temporal relations which bind the causal conditions to one another, and the temporal relation which ties the causal conditions to their effect. My intention is to draw out the startling implications of this idea, and then to replace it with a theory of causal relationships which avoids these difficulties and provides a more viable foundation for the claim that causes will always produce their effects.

Some preliminary distinctions are in order. In particular, we require a clear statement of the difference between causal relationships, and spatial and temporal relationships. The causal relationship is best defined, I think, as a single, continuous process in which one or more causal conditions are modified in some way, in the moment when all of a set of causal conditions are brought into proper spatial and temporal range of one another: the effect occurs not merely when the causal conditions are assembled, but because they are assembled. "Process," in this context at least, means a continuous movement or development which is controlled, directed and unified by a principle. In the case of causal relationships, the directing principles are causal laws. Spatial and temporal relationships are very different from causal relationships. They are not processes, because they move or develop in no particular direction, nor are they controlled by a principle. In the absence of these factors, spatial and temporal relationships have no unity other than what is lent by the fact that they are conjunctions in one space and one time. Any distracted moment in a lifetime is an example of a mere spatial and temporal relationship. There is the contiguity of the objects which are seen and touched, and the succession of sounds, smells, and feelings. The first moments in a foreign city are like this, and the hallmark of the experience is the externality of the related factors. Each one brushes past the others and has no effect upon them, as they have none on it.

If we define *accidental conjunction* as that conjunction in which the nonoccurrence or modification of one conjunct has no consequences for the existence or character of the other conjuncts, we see that mere relationship in space and time is the most pervasive kind of accidental conjunction.

Let us consider some event in terms of these distinctions: putting a flaming match to a sheet of newspaper which then burns is a satisfactory example. This is obviously a causal relationship, and, in terms of what has been said above, this means that the causal conditions are responsible for the occurrence of the effect; it occurs *because* they have been satisfied. Many philosophers are in sharp disagreement with this interpretation. Adopting the assumption which I have accepted up to this time, but now reject, they argue that the spatial and temporal relations of the causes are the only factors in a set of causal conditions which are significant for the analysis of causality, and they say that the "because" which I have emphasized above expresses nothing more than the fact that the assembly of a set of causal conditions is temporally antecedent to the occurrence of the effect. This analysis is an attempt to reduce causal relationships to the status of spatial and temporal relationships, and the following objections are intended by me to prove that it is an unsatisfactory characterization of both of the two stages of a causal relationship.

1] It cannot be that completion of a set of causal conditions is exhaustively described for purposes of an analysis of causality if reference is only made to the spatial and temporal relations of the causal conditions. If this were a satisfactory account, we could expect the newspaper to burn even if an unlighted match were substituted for the lighted one of our example. Of course, the paper would not burn, and this shows that something over and above the proximity of the causal conditions is required if an effect is to be produced. The reductionist retort is likely to be that I have distorted their view by making no provision for the fact of motion, and hence by supposing that they offer a merely static description of the spatial and temporal relations of causal conditions. It is true that the relative motion of the causal conditions has not been explicitly considered, but it is not true that a reference to motion is enough to save the reductionist analysis. An ice cube hurled at a sheet of paper may cause the paper to tear, but it will not make the paper burn. Changes in the relative positions of causal agencies are still not sufficient to assure that an effect will be produced.

2] The relation between a set of causal conditions and its effect cannot be reduced to the fact that the assembly of the causal conditions is antecedent to the occurrence of the effect. There are two ways of proving that this cannot be a valid account: (a) Let us suppose that temporal succession is the only relation tying a set of causal conditions to an effect. This identifies the causal conditions and the effect as accidental conjuncts, and it entails that the occurrence of the effect is an independent phenomenon which owes nothing to the interaction of the set of causal conditions. Under the circumstances, there is no reason why an explosion should occur when a torch is set to dynamite. The explosion may occur one time, but *it should be just as likely that something else might happen.* Indeed, it should be possible that anything could follow upon completion of the set of causal conditions, or even when the set was not completely assembled, and it would be miraculous that explosions do in fact always occur when a heat source, oxygen, and dynamite are in immediate proximity to one another. This, it seems to me, is a *reductio ad absurdum* of the claim that succession is all that matters in cause-and-effect relations; (b) This objection takes logical precedence over the one just above, and it also is in the form of a *reductio.* Consider the matter from the vantage point of the effect. It has occurred, but the only factors related to it have been reduced in status; they are merely its temporal antecedents, and they have no responsibility for its occurrence or for the character it has. In these circumstances, there is no factor which could have been sufficient to have produced the effect, and, in the absence of a sufficient condition, the effect should not have occurred. But of course it has occurred, and we therefore deny the assumption which prompted us to suppose that it should not have done so: the assembly of a set of causal conditions cannot be related to an effect merely as an event which is antecedent to the occurrence of the effect.

These are the implications, and the objections, to a theory which reduces causal relationships to the spatial and temporal relations which are their barest formal supports. Experience shows that particular effects are produced by some kinds of things but not by others, and yet, this theory abstracts from the *material identity* of the causal conditions, and supposes that anonymous and undifferentiated units can be sufficient to produce the variety of effects which do occur in the world. Such a theory cannot begin to clarify the nature of causal relationships, because it regards causal conditions as quasi-mathematical entities whose only role is to mark the boundaries of a spatial and temporal relationship. One is perhaps reminded by this objection of the Aristotelian critics who argued that seventeenth century physicists could not account for the diversity in our experience of the world so long as the physicists supposed that shape, motion and extension are the only properties of physical objects. There is a similarity between the present objection and that older one, but there is also a considerable difference. Philosophers who reduce causal relationships to spatial and temporal relationships are far more extreme than the physicists, past and present, who accept a distinction between primary and secondary qualities. The philosophers who analyze causality in this way are denying that *any* property is relevant to the fact that an object performs as a causal condition. Physicists can argue that the interaction of causes having certain primary qualities is sufficient to make for the variety of effects which occur in the world, but philosophers who entirely disregard all of the properties of causal conditions cannot tell us how any effect can ever be produced in this conceptual universe of theirs.

And similarly, philosophers who regard causal conditions and effects as mere temporal conjuncts have obliterated essential formal aspects of the causal relationship. As I shall argue, provision has to be made for the facts of *production* and *existential dependence* if we are to distinguish causal relationships from accidental conjunctions in space and time.

Ib. 2] (d) vi. *Restatement of claim that complete sets of causal conditions will always produce effects as an assertion that these sets of causal conditions must produce their effects; vii. Two objections, and replies to them; viii. Hume's tacit acceptance of effects-must-occur theory.*

Generally, the fundamental difficulty with this reductionist theory is its failure to note the differences between a static, geometrical view of causality and the causal relationships which occur in the world. We are required to observe these differences if there is to be a theory of causal relationships which will support the claim that effects will always occur when causal conditions are satisfied. I suggest that the following arguments do provide for all of the important categorical factors in both stages of the causal relationship.

In analyzing the first stage, we are obliged to distinguish a set of causal conditions from a random grouping of accidental conjuncts in space and time. The essential difference seems to be this: In mere spatial and temporal relationships, spatial and temporal relations proper are the only significant factor; we want to know how close or how far things are from one another, but that is all. Our interest is purely geometrical, or else chronological. With causal relationships, however, we also want to know what *kinds* of things have these spatial and temporal relations to one another. Production of the effect requires that causal conditions should come into spatial and temporal range of one another, but their proximity, or even collision, is not enough to bring about a change in one or more of them. The effect occurs, because things of the right kinds are collected together. This is to state the obvious fact that things in the world regularly divide themselves into two groups; those contributing to the production of a specific change, and those not. We express our understanding of this fact every time we are given a job to perform. We prepare for the effort by locating the minds or objects which are adapted to producing the desired effect. Only subsequently do we arrange them in the proper spatial and temporal relations to one another.

Recognition that causes are things of certain kinds makes it very much easier for us to isolate the factors distinguishing cause and effect from temporal relations. The factors we require are implicit, I believe, in the notions of causal sufficiency and necessity. These complementary notions have already been discussed from the standpoint of the theory that cause-and-effect relations are nothing more than temporal relations, but now I want to give them a second explication which will supersede and justify that earlier one.

Causal sufficiency is the notion that a complete set of causal conditions is capable of bringing about a change, and does in fact *produce* it. The effect is not a random occurrence, only casually related to its causal conditions. The very opposite is true; antecedent causal conditions are responsible for its occurrence and the character which it has. Their affinities one for another are such that the effect naturally occurs when they are assembled. "Affinities" is not to be interpreted as meaning that causes have secret yearnings for one another. It only points to the fact that things are qualified to join with some, but not with all, others for the production of a specific effect.

Understanding causal sufficiency in this way, we no longer regard it as the property of a class of occurrences. This is the interpretation which I gave to it above when I suggested that the notion of causal sufficiency could be defined with the statement that, when causes occur effects will also occur. Now, however, we are free to say that causal sufficiency is a factor in the relation of a particular set of causal conditions and its effect: they are sufficient to bring about the effect; they produce it.

The notion of causal sufficiency treats the causal relationship from the side of the causal conditions, and the perspective shifts when we take up the idea of causal necessity. We consider this notion from the side of the effect. The clue leading to the discovery of this idea is the fact that changes do not turn up anywhere and at any time. They are tied to the sets of causal conditions responsible for their occurrence, and causal necessity is apparently the fact that effects, produced by their causal conditions, are in turn *dependent* upon them for their occurrence and character. As in the instance of causal sufficiency, we are no longer required to understand the idea of necessary connection in terms of constant conjunction. Causal necessity is the same as the dependence of effects upon their causal conditions, and this is a factor in every causal relationship.

Understanding causal sufficiency and necessity in these terms, we find that constant conjunctions of causes and effects are less mysterious than is made out by philosophers who espouse frequency theories to account for these regularities. We are now in a position to argue that particular sets of causal conditions regularly produce certain effects, because minds and objects of certain kinds naturally produce those effects when they meet one another. And similarly, the effects only occur when they do, because their dependence upon these sets of causal conditions makes it naturally impossible for them to occur in other situations. In these ways, the ideas of production and dependence validate the claims of the effects-will-always-occur theory, and what is more, they convert it into the stronger claim that a set of causal conditions *must always* produce an effect so long as there are no external factors preventing its occurrence.

The assertion that causes must always produce their effects is often dismissed out of hand, because of a failure to distinguish two significantly different objections to it. One objection holds that this claim is mistaken, because cause and effect relations are merely relations of succession, and because this is too casual a relation to suppose that causes and effects will always be tied by it. This is the theory which has been discussed in detail. The second reason for doubting that causes must always produce effects is entirely different from the first. It does not deny that there is causal sufficiency and necessity in the world, or that the constancy of cause and effect relations is assured by the facts of production and dependence. It does question, however, whether the world must always be constituted as it is. This objection supposes that there might be a radical upset in nature such that causal laws as we presently know them would be rendered inoperative. In that event, a set of causal conditions which had invariably produced a certain effect in the past would not produce it any longer, and the claim that causal conditions must always produce effects would be false.

These two responses to the effects-must-always-occur theory are not equally plausible. The first one has already been rejected, because it holds (mistakenly) that the world *as presently constituted* has no formal constituents beyond its spatial and temporal relations. The other objection must be reckoned a serious challenge, and I want to discuss it in a little detail.

There are two forms which this hypothesis may take. One statement of it holds that it is at least possible that the world might experience a partial or complete upset which would occur in a moment or a short span of time, and would be caused by an agency outside of our universe. This suggestion may not be perfectly intelligible, because it might be impossible to clarify the manner in which the postulated external agency could be related to the world, or to tell how it could happen that the agency was suddenly sufficient to cause a sharp upset in our world when it had not been sufficient to do so previously. These difficulties prompt the formulation of a second version of the hypothesis. This time it is argued that the possible upset in our causal laws might be subtle and slow rather than quick and violent; and that rather than being imposed upon the system from without, the upset might be caused by an evolutionary tendency that has always been present and active in our world. This second statement of the hypothesis could take any of several forms. It could be argued that eons, centuries, or just days are required before we notice that causal conditions are producing effects slightly different each time. Furthermore, it would have to be stipulated whether the change in the natural order moves equably, is alternately accelerated and depressed, moves pendulum-like, or whatever. Given any combination of these variations, this second statement of the hypothesis is ideally verifiable by empirical methods. It should be possible for scientists making observations over a lengthy period to notice a systematic variation in the effects being produced by sets of causal conditions. Or, presuming that change is continuous and that experimental techniques were sufficiently advanced, it should be possible to discern this change in even a very short period of time.

Proper evaluation of these two statements of the hypothesis is not our present concern, but I do want to outline the consequences that the truth of either would have for the claim that causes must always produce their effects. The possibility that causal laws would be radically upset in a brief period of time admits that causal laws would be operative up to the time of the upset, and therefore, that a complete set of causal conditions must always produce effects up to the moment of cataclysm. Afterwards, there might be no causal laws and chaos would result, or there might be a return to stability, and new causal laws would make that nascent world as orderly as our present one. The second possibility is more difficult to square with our theory of causality. Causal law statements accommodated to this hypothesis would refer to a range of time, and would say that a particular set of causal conditions will produce effects tending to vary systematically in the course of that period. Finally, when the effect produced by a set of causal conditions had changed out of all recognition from the effect which early ancestors had known, scientists and laymen could look back and deny that sets of causal conditions had always to produce the same effect.

In view of the possibility that one of the forms of this hypothesis might turn out to be correct, it should not be said flatly that effects must always occur when a set of causal conditions is complete. Nonetheless, provisos which we are required to add to the effects-must-always-occur theory do not justify the skepticism of empiricists who worry that the future might not be like the past. So long as the world remains constituted as it is, so long that is as we have causal interaction among substances of the kinds known to scientists and laymen, there is no likelihood that causal conditions will fail to produce their effects. Once our experimental techniques have shown that a particular relationship is a causal one, we are assured by the metaphysical analyses of substance and the interaction of substances that the relevant effect will be produced as often as substances of the proper kinds are assembled. Empiricists dispute this not because they fear the radical or evolutionary upset which I have just discussed, but rather because of what must be called a shallow understanding of substance and the causal relationship.

There should be a last word about the extent to which this discussion of production and dependence is supposed to be an exposition of Hume. So far as I can discover, there are no passages in which Hume explicitly endorses my essentialist conclusions. However, Hume does write of abstract ideas, and of the association of ideas in general, as if he were conceiving of these relations in terms of a theory of causality which is like the one for which I have argued. Thus, Hume is pleased to discover that a single, determinate idea can represent a number of other ideas in thought, but there is no suggestion that this sign is believed to be merely antecedent to the represented ideas when they finally appear as objects of reflection. The sign is a particular kind of idea; Hume supposes, for example, that the idea representing all triangles will itself be the idea of a triangle. Some other idea could serve the purpose, but it is clear that whatever idea is finally associated with the represented triangles as their sign, it will be an idea with a determinate content. Similarly, it is not any sort of need of reflection that prompts us to think of triangles, but a particular sort of need, and not every mind that can think them but only a mind which (on my interpolation) has acquired a nonintrospectable mental state.

All three of these factors are causal conditions, and they

are together responsible for causing the represented ideas to appear as objects of conscious reflection. They function in this way because of their identity and their contiguity, both, and not merely because of the latter. A different intellectual need and a different sign conceived at the same time as these were conceived would have prompted the appearance in thought of ideas different from those which did occur. And in turn, the conceiving of formerly represented ideas is dependent upon the assembly of the appropriate causal conditions; in the absence of any one of the relevant conditions, the ideas do not appear in thought. This is made very clear in the passage quoted above: it was said that required ideas will not occur to thought so long as one of the causal conditions, the faculties, is imperfect. Arguing in this way, Hume anticipates, whether he is conscious of it or not, all of the distinctions that are important for a theory which argues that spatial and temporal relations are not the only significant factors in a causal relationship.

There is one last bit of evidence for the claim that Hume sometimes adopts a theory of causality like the one I have proposed. Hume insists that minds have powers, but, as I shall try to prove in the discussion that immediately follows, the inference that things have powers is not required unless we are trying to account for the fact that some kind of thing is qualified to be a causal condition for making or suffering a certain change, while other sorts of things are not so qualified. This is another of the motivations behind Hume's inference that minds have powers. By inferring that a mind has a power, he succeeds in explaining how it is that this mind is able to think in ways that are not open to other minds. Here again the emphasis is upon causal conditions which are things of certain kinds; the mere spatial and temporal relations of the causal conditions receive little or no stress. This is surely evidence for the view that Hume was of two opinions. His skepticism is often tempered by a realization that there is no accounting for the fact of change if we refuse to admit the efficacy of powers and kinds.

Ib. 2] (e) *Dispositions qualifying substances to be causal conditions; i. Dispositions defined as real potentialities which qualify minds and objects to be causal agencies; ii. Supposed objections to real potentiality; iii. The causal-law theory as proof that dispositions are real potentialities.*

v. This brings us to the discussion of powers themselves. Hume has this to say of powers:

> It may justly be concluded, that *power* has always a reference to its *exercise*, either actual or probable, and that we consider a person as endow'd with an ability when we find from past experience, that 'tis probable, or at least possible he may exert it. And indeed . . . nothing can be more likely of itself, without any further reasoning than that power consists in the possibility or probability of any action, as discover'd by experience and the practice of the world.[18]

As I understand it, this passage either states or implies everything of importance about dispositional properties; Hume tells us how to proceed in analyzing powers, and he defines them. His method is the one which realists, including myself, normally adopt: we acknowledge that there is change (Hume writes of "exercise" and "action") and we then infer that things which have suffered or initiated a change must have been endowed with powers which enabled them to act as they did. The powers, themselves, are described as the possibilities or probabilities (I shall refer to them as real potentialities) which qualify things having them to perform in certain ways. Regarding an exercise or an action as an effect, we may interpret Hume as saying that powers are the real potentialities which qualify minds to act as causal conditions. Now generalizing his analysis to include physical objects as well as minds, we may define powers as the real potentialities which qualify the minds and objects having them for participation in causal relationships.

Nothing in this definition conflicts with our everyday talk about the world. Notice that we frequently ascribe great potentialities to things like race horses and athletes, and that we talk of the realization of an innate power on occasions when supplementary conditions such as favorable humidity and a good track combine to help a man turn in a record breaking performance. We acknowledge possession of inferior potentialities when we say that a gale at our backs would not be sufficient to make us do as well.

There are numerous examples like these, but there are also many philosophers who regard this familiar talk as typical ordinary language indiscretion. These are philosophers who believe that the realist definition is implausible and unnecessary. They are likely to ask why anyone should suppose that dispositions are real potentialities, with some peculiar status in being, when dispositions are perfectly well understood in terms of an analysis of causal laws. The answer, I think, is that the causal law, reductionist analysis of powers is not perfect or even fairly satisfactory, and, indeed, I can best demonstrate the truth of the realist definition by showing that it takes account of a crucial distinction neglected by the causal law theory.

As a preliminary to the argument, we require an outline of this analysis. The causal law theorists, as I shall call them, accept the common-sense view that ascription of a dispositional property commits us to believing that some mind or object is able to contribute to the production of a change. However, these philosophers disparage the popular assumption that dispositions are properties which things possess even while no change is being suffered or effected by them. They argue instead that having a disposition is equivalent to falling within the determination of a causal law.

In order to comprehend this point, we have to remember that it is the function of causal laws to fix the relations of causes and effects, and that any particular law determines that some complete set of causal conditions will produce a specific change as its natural effect. The relation of a causal law to particular substances will then be as follows. A mind or object falls within the determination of a causal law when it is an instance of one of the kinds of substances whose assembly must, in accordance with the determination of the law, result in the production of a certain effect. A substance whose actions are thus determined will contribute to the production of an effect whenever the other relevant causal conditions are assembled. On this analysis, having a power to initiate or suffer a change is identical with being the sort of mind or object which contributes to bringing about that change when the other members of a set of causal conditions are present. Dispositions are not strange properties carried about by minds and objects in anticipation that they will meet things which are likewise equipped to assist in producing a change; there is only the causal law determining that things of certain kinds will act appropriately when circumstances require.

Ideally, this analysis is tailored to the dispositions of things which belong to classes having an indefinite number of members. The reason for this is that causal laws are thought to be universal in scope; [14] the membership of the class of events covered by a causal law should not be limited to the events in any one space-time region of the universe. This feature of causal laws complicates the analysis of dispositional properties, because there are many dispositions which appear to be the unique properties of individuals. Psychologists, for example, try to cure neuroses which are highly idiosyncratic. It is true that a man having a compulsive tendency will act predictably if his circumstances are carefully modified, but this not withstanding, we hesitate to say that the factor controlling his actions is a causal law for the reason that this factor determines how one man alone shall respond. Causal law theorists have to choose between two ways of accommodating these special cases to the requirements of their analysis. They may liberalize the requirements for being a causal law, and say that a law may cover a class of events having only one member, or, more in vogue, they may propose that the psychologist should try to show that the individual's conduct is an instance of a common sort of behavior, and that it displays only slight and accountable variations from the norm.

There is a second feature of dispositions to be accounted for, and in this instance the notion of universal scope is an asset to the causal-law analysis. The characteristic openness of powers is the feature that I have in mind. This openness is pre-supposed when we say that a mind or object is qualified to initiate or undergo a change without stipulating when or where the change will occur, or the specific identity of the causal conditions whose satisfaction will be sufficient to make it occur: thus, some dogs are likely to bark anytime, anywhere, and at nearly any provocation. Causal-law theorists interpret this aspect of dispositional properties by reminding us that the force of a causal law is not limited to any particular space-time region. Minds and objects having certain powers, which is to say, falling within the determination of a law, will help to produce changes whenever and wherever supplementary conditions are assembled.

With these outstanding problems settled, the reductionist is prepared to argue that his causal-law analysis satisfactorily accounts for all powers and capacities. Dispositional properties, he claims, are not any kind of property; least of all are they real potentialities. Talk about powers is taken for nothing more than a kind of conceptual shorthand for more complicated talk about causal laws.

This attempted reductionist theory of powers is reminiscent of the "shall-if" and "should have-if" analysis of "can" and "could have" sentences with Austin criticizes for entailing that things have no powers and abilities unless they are suffering or initiating a change. The similarity between these two reductionist analyses is an expression of the fact that the theory which I have just outlined has two forms, and that Austin has attacked one of them. One statement of the theory first argues that dispositional properties should be understood in terms of causal laws, and then goes on to claim that causal laws, themselves, should be reductively analyzed by way of reference to causal-law statements. This is the version of the theory discussed by Austin. In its other form, the theory provides a reductive analysis of powers like the one described above, but argues that causal laws, at any rate, have some kind of reality in being rather than in language.

The striking objection to both forms of the causal-law analysis of powers is that they both apparently fail to satisfy the commonsense notion that things do have powers even while they are inactive. It is conceivable of course that this popular view is mistaken, and in the second chapter I shall assume that it is, in order to give fuller consideration to the "shall-if" statement analysis of powers. For the present, however, I want to suppose that failure to accommodate the common-sense notion is evidence against any theory of dispositional properties. Making this assumption, I want to ask whether the two forms of the causal-law analysis are equally objectionable from the standpoint of common sense. It seems to me that they are not, and that the difference between them is owing to the fact that one statement of the theory offers a reductionist account of causal laws, while the other supposes that the laws are real. The former approach denies the reality of both dispositions and causal laws, nor does it make any reference to other factors upon which to peg the reality of powers during those times when things are inactive. There is nothing in this statement of the causal-law analysis which makes any concession to the common-sense view. By contrast, however, the other statement of the causal-law theory admits that causal laws have reality during the times when minds and objects covered by the laws are not producing changes. Supposing that powers should be analyzed by way of reference to causal laws, it follows from the reality of laws enduring when things covered by them are inactive that powers themselves do endure throughout these times. When we interpret it in this way, the second form of the causal-law analysis escapes the criticism which Austin has made of the other form of the theory, and deserves further attention. In particular, I want to determine the sort of reality attributed by this theory to causal laws.

The man who believes that causal laws are real is likely to justify himself by calling our attention to the orderliness that we find in experience. He will point out that changes of certain kinds are invariably produced by particular sets of causal conditions, and, ruling out the possibility of a colossal and continuing miracle, he will argue that there must be enduring laws which determine that causes should only, and invariably, produce specific effects. When asked to tell us about the status in being of the laws, this philosopher is likely to canvass and reject three possibilities before he chooses a fourth one. First of all, it is evident to him that causal laws are not objects of perception; they are not observable, material particulars. Second, he sees that the causal law should not be equated with the sum of occasions when the causal conditions covered by the law have produced their effect; this would be a category mistake, confusing the law which fixes the relation of causes and effects with the particular instances when an effect is produced by a set of causal conditions. A symptom of this category difference is the fact that the law determines how a certain relation might hold in an infinite number of cases, while the number of particular occurrences of the causal relationship controlled by the law is always finite. Third, he might regard causal laws as exemplars of natural order with the status of Platonic ideas or concepts in the mind of God. But this alternative is soon rejected, because it entails all the ambiguities of the Platonic theory of participation: it is not clear how ideas which exist in a sphere of intelligible being can determine the relations of causes and effects in the material world. With the drawbacks of these three possibilities in mind, a philosopher who maintains the reality of causal laws has the problem of saving the categorical difference between causal laws and their instances, while finding a place for these laws in the material world.

Arguing now as a causal realist, I suggest that we can solve this problem in the following way. We begin by acknowledging that there is a correlation between the changes which substances produce and the kinds of properties they have. We interpret this correlation as an expression of the orderliness which is imposed upon experience by causal laws, and also, as possible evidence of the status in being which these laws possess. There may be significance in the fact that this correlation pairs the effects produced against causes having properties of certain kinds; these properties may be a factor in determining which effects must be produced by substances acting as causal agencies. It is conceivable, after all, that there might have been a different correlation. We might have discovered that the identity of the effects produced varies uniformly with the time of year and the place where they occur.

A simple argument confirms our suspicions. We suppose that the kinds of properties possessed by causal agencies are not a factor in determining what effects the causes must produce, and we deduce from this assumption that there should be a random variation in the effects produced by particular sets of causal conditions. That this does follow from our premise is evident, I think, if we remember that our assumption declares that the kinds of properties possessed by causal conditions have *no* part in determining the identity of their effects. In these circumstances, it would be nothing less than miraculous if a particular set of causal conditions always did produce the same effect. Instead of the correlation between effects and causes of certain kinds, there would be a chaos in which any sort of effect might occur when a set of causal conditions was assembled. It is true that events might be correlated in the alternative manner suggested above, or in some other and even more obscure fashion, but nonetheless, where order to us human beings means that effects of certain kinds are produced by causes of certain kinds, the assumption which we are considering entails a disorderly universe.

There is just one last hedge which might be suggested by someone who favors this assumption. It is possible, as he would tell us, that the assumption is true, and that chaos is nonetheless forestalled by a continuing miracle. Unfortunately, the reference to miracles is always a patchwork explanation which no one is obliged to adopt so long as he has an even fractionally more plausible account to give. In the present instance, we have an alternative explanation which is much better than marginally preferable, for it is coherent and wholly intelligible to say that the kinds of properties possessed by causal agencies are significant factors in determining what effects the causes must produce.

At this point, the realist has to specify the *extent* to which the efficacy of causal laws is conditioned by the fact that causal conditions have properties of certain kinds; is this merely an important consideration, or is it the decisive one. As it happens, the kinds of properties possessed by causes are the principal factor which has to be taken into account in analyzing causal laws. By elaborating upon the notion of kinds (Aristotle spoke of formal causes), we can solve both of the problems which normally embarrass realist theories of causal laws.

We provide for the normative aspect of these laws by reinterpreting the claim that causal laws determine that sets of causal conditions must produce certain effects. Taking care to assure that our reinterpretation clarifies the origins of this normative principle, we account for the efficacy of causal laws by saying that the members of a set of causal conditions must interact as they do, for the reason that they are things of certain kinds. This way of characterizing the situation preserves the distinction between the normative principle and its instances; it follows from our statement that the same effect must be produced whenever the relevant causal agencies are combined.

The second problem requiring a solution was that of finding a place for causal laws in the material world, but our success in locating the origins of the normative aspect of the laws makes it evident that this has become the problem of accounting for the reality of kinds. The only plausible solution to this problem of which I am aware is the Aristotelian view that kinds are *universalia in rebus*. No other theory does justice to the facts of experience while avoiding the extremes of Platonic realism on the one hand, and an atomism of monadic particulars on the other. If we analyze the reality of kinds as Aristotle would have us do, we have to deny that kinds and causal laws are existent *entities* of any sort. This, however, is not to say that kinds and causal laws are mere creatures of reason. Physical objects and minds, or atomic particles, may well be the only things that exist, but their bare existential particularity is not all that is important in them. This is evident when we recall the aforementioned correlation between the properties of a substance and the effects it produces. We may argue that substance is fundamental in nature, but we have to agree that there are various categorical factors whose reality cannot be denied if we are to give a thorough analysis of the being and activity of substance. Kinds and causal laws are two of these factors. Their reality is the reality of substances having diverse properties, and in the instance of causal laws, it is the reality of substances having, because of their properties, to produce certain effects when supplementary conditions are assembled.

This characterization of the reality of causal laws will strike many people as unsatisfactory. As I am describing it, the reality of the laws is the reality of substances like tables and chairs, and yet others will suppose that causal laws have an entirely different status in being. With a Platonizing inclination, they will conceive of causal laws after the manner of our causal law statements, and they will argue that the reality of causal laws must be the reality of principles having a magisterial form like that of counterfactual statements. And so, they would have us believe that there are exemplars known to reason which somehow resemble the proposition that, for example, if sufficient heat is applied, water will boil. While recognizing that this is an unsympathetic representation of other people's views, I suggest that my summary is not so remote from the view that philosophers must be adopting if they seriously intend that causal laws have reality in some way other than by way of the substances whose activities they determine. I admit that I do not understand what sort of reality this would be, and therefore, I suppose for the sake of the discussion which follows that the reality of causal laws is to be understood in terms of the reality possessed by substances.

Ib. 2](e) iv. *Proof that dispositions cannot be reductively analyzed by reference to reality of causal laws;* v. *Justification of definition of powers as real potentialities qualifying substances to participate in causal relationships;* vi. *All members of a set of causal conditions must have these powers;* (f) *Logical relation of potentialities to causal relationship;* (g) *Some remaining problems.*

This brings us to the question relative to which all of the foregoing is mere prologue. While I agree, subject to a reservation to be mentioned below, that causal laws are real in the way just specified, I doubt that this theory of causal laws is able to support an acceptable reductionist theory of dispositional properties. Consider how dispositions are regarded by this version of the causal-law analysis. While we ordinarily conceive of powers as potentialities for initiating or suffering a change, the reductionist tells us that this is a myth. Dispositional language, he argues, obscures the fact that things have dispositions just to the extent that their behavior, present or prospective, is determined by a causal law. But as it now appears, there are causal laws in nature just insofar as there are individual existents which are distinguished from one another by properties such as their sizes, weights and molecular structures. It is this conception of causal laws which highlights the problem. The properties which I have named identify something as an actual. This means that the reduction of dispositional properties to talk about causal laws eventually entails that we have reduced them to the properties which constitute the actuality of minds and objects. Things certainly do continue to have their shapes, weight, and, I think, their mental states during the times when they are not helping to produce changes, and, to this extent, we have justified the suspicion that this version of the causal-law analysis of powers does ultimately square with the common-sense view that things have powers even while they are not acting. Nonetheless, this account reduces potentiality to actuality; and the failure to observe this ground-level categorical distinction makes the causal-law reductionist analysis an unsatisfactory account of dispositional properties.

To prove that potentiality cannot be reduced to actuality, let us consider the powers of any mind or physical substance. The version of the causal-law reductionist analysis which we are considering tells us that this thing must suffer or effect some change in the presence of supplementary causal conditions, because of having certain physical properties, or in the case of minds, certain nonintrospectable mental states or brain states. However, we can easily imagine a world in which this thing, with the exact same molecular structure or brain structure, contributes to the production of changes utterly different from the changes it suffers or effects in this world. Though having the molecular structure of an acid, it turns litmus paper into a sulfurous gas. Introduced to this novel state of affairs, we would say, I think, that the solution has changed. It must have, because, as we reason, a difference in the effect produced presupposes a difference in the antecedent causal conditions. Just what sort of change can this have been? Certainly not a change in the properties which mark the solution as an actual, because it is stipulated that these properties are the same in our world and the imaginary one. Rather—and there appears to be no way of avoiding this inference—the solution has changed because one of its dispositional properties has changed, and the litmus has undergone a similar modification.

Our conceptual experiment reopens the question of the status of these dispositional properties; these can no longer be analyzed in terms of the properties marking the actuality of litmus and an acidic solution: how could they be when the powers have changed while these properties have not? It must be true, therefore, that the powers are distinguishable from the properties which are responsible for the actuality of the causal conditions, and are, moreover, a different sort of property. Properties which do not mark the actuality of things must be real potentialities; there are no other kinds of properties. This establishes, as I set out to establish, that the causal-law analysis of dispositional properties must be rejected for having tried to reduce potentiality to actuality.

Two criticisms of this argument are likely to come to mind. The first one is that I have based a claim about our world upon the seemingly irrelevant possibility of our being able to imagine a different world. This objection is validly directed at some conceptual experiments, but not to all, the crucial difference being the uses made of the experiments. Some philosophers ask us to imagine a world different from our world in an important respect, and they subsequently begin to talk as if our world were identical with that different, imaginary one. This is the procedure by which Hume tries illegitimately to justify his most skeptical utterances about causality. He asks us to imagine a world in which some events have no causes, and then proceeds to argue as if that were our world. (His argument will be considered in detail in the next section.) This is a different mode of analysis from the one that is applied above. I have not attributed to our world any factor native to an imaginary universe. In the argument I have proposed, a world, different in a specific respect from our own, is imagined in order to provide a basis for comparison. The object of the comparison is to direct our attention to a categorical distinction which is already present in our world though it is in danger of going unnoticed.

The second objection to my argument regards its assumptions: The argument begins with the stipulation that we should imagine a world in which causal conditions produce a different effect from the one which they produce in our world. This stipulation presupposes that causal conditions can be distinguished from their effect, and moreover, that it is plausible to assume that a set of causal conditions can be *separated* from its normal effect. The argument now goes on to make a tacit appeal to the assumption that causes producing an effect have dispositions which qualify them to produce it, and the claim is made that causal conditions producing different effects must have different powers. It has already been assumed that the two sets of causal conditions are identical with respect to the properties which constitute the actuality of the substances, and therefore, it appears safe to conclude that dispositions must be real potentialities. But as a matter of fact, it is not safe, because the first of the assumptions outlined above is partly mistaken; it is true that causal conditions can be distinguished from their effects, but it is not true that they can be separated from those effects. It is rather the case that the natures of the members of a set of causal conditions are such that these substances could never produce any effect other than the one they do produce in our world. The misconception that they could produce other effects precisely reflects the way in which we learn about the relation of causes and effects. Lacking the insight of an omniscient being, we are forced to wait upon experience to show us which effects will be produced by sets of causal agencies. We do ultimately come to regard the causal conditions as sufficient and necessary for the production of the effects, but we do not outgrow the suspicion that events could have been otherwise, and that other effects might have resulted from the completion of these sets of causal conditions. As it stands in nature, however, there is no basis for this suspicion, and there is no justification for so much as imagining that minds and objects could retain their identities while suffering a modification of the powers which qualify them to produce changes: being the kinds of things they are, minds and objects must produce just the changes we find them producing in this world.

Consequently (the objection continues), we see that the argument for real potentiality depends upon the device of illegitimately separating causes from the effects they produce. This separation has been required in order to make it plausible to compare identical causal agencies as they produce first one effect and then a different one. Given such a state of affairs, we do have to account for the difference in the effects produced, and where properties constituting the actuality of the causes are thought to be identical in the two instances, it is reasonable to suppose that there must be a previously unacknowledged difference in the causes. As demonstrated, however, this entire chain of reasoning is groundless. It is not permissible to suppose that genuine and imaginary acid have different effects, and to argue that they must therefore have different powers. But remember now that the only excuse for arguing that the two acids must have real potentialities has been that the acids have different powers and that where properties-like mass are identical, the powers must be real potentialities. Having justified our proscription of this talk about different powers, we are free to conclude that nothing has been said to convince us that powers are real potentialities. Indeed, real potentiality has been exposed as an unnecessary positum. Powers are identical with the properties which determine how things shall exist as actuals.

This is evidently the more serious of the two objections to my argument. Nonetheless, I do not find this objection convincing, and speaking on behalf of the Absolute, whose criticism this is supposed to be, I doubt that he would be impressed by it. The conceptual separability of causes and effects is surely the fulcrum of my argument, but the argument does not rely upon our ignorance of the true force of the sufficiency and necessity in a causal relationship. One can admit that an all-knowing being would regard every true statement about our world as analytic, but this would not decide the important issue, which is whether the analyticity of statements about the relations of causes and effects in this world precludes the chance that there might be other worlds in which causal conditions have properties like the molecular structures of causal conditions we know, but nonetheless produces different effects. The answer is that it would *not* be impossible for this other world to exist. Not impossible, means that it does not violate the principle of contradiction to suppose that there could be worlds of this kind. The principle of contradiction certainly is not a principle of existence: the success of an idea in satisfying the principle is not sufficient to make for the existence of the object of that idea. But yet, satisfaction of the principle is a necessary condition for existence, and an idea which satisfies the principle thereby establishes the minimum warrant for our saying that it is the idea of a possible existent. The imaginary world which I proposed embodies no contradiction, and, therefore, it meets this minimum condition for existence. It may satisfy no other conditions, and in particular none of the physical laws which control the relations of causes and effects in our world; but in spite of this it does meet the primitive condition for existence, and we consequently refute the charge that it is mere ignorance which allows us to imagine a world that is different from our own. The omniscient being must acknowledge that this world is a logical possibility, and also that causal law statements which are analytic in our world would be false in that imaginary one.

This justifies us in reaffirming the view that dispositional properties are real potentialities. Moreover, we are now in a position to understand why it is that no attempt to give a reductive causal law analysis of dispositions can ever succeed. There are two factors to be considered: the respective functions of powers and laws, and the manner in which powers and laws are real. We have all of the distinctions which are required to prove that potentiality has logical priority over causal laws on both counts.

First with respect to function. The function of causal laws is to determine that specific effects shall be produced whenever all of a set of causal conditions are assembled. The function of potentialities, however, is to qualify substances for participation in the causal relationships which are fixed by causal laws. The question of logical priority is easily settled in this instance, for if there were no dispositions qualifying objects to serve as causal conditions, it would be gratuitous to hold that these substances must produce effects. Substances have to be capable of acting in certain ways before it can be true to say that they must act in these ways.

Passing now to the issue of the reality of causal laws and powers, we recall that the reality of the laws has been described as the reality of substances having properties of certain kinds. As we must now agree, the phrase "properties of certain kinds" wants reinterpreting. The phrase cannot merely refer to properties such as mass and weight, for, as we have seen, interacting substances produce one effect rather than another because of having certain powers as well as because of having properties such as mass. "Properties of certain kinds" must therefore refer to properties which mark the actuality of substances and *also* to real potentialities. But if this is true, we cannot deny that the reality of powers is logically prior to the reality of causal laws. The reality of the laws is the reality of substances of particular kinds, but minds and objects are substances of one kind or another only by virtue of the fact that they have some properties, including dispositional properties, rather than others.

The idea that dispositions can be reductively analyzed by way of reference to causal laws seems to me to be the most serious challenge to the claim that dispositions are real potentialities, and yet, as I think this prolonged discussion has established, it will not do to say that talk about powers is merely an elliptical way of talking about causal laws.

Our original definition of powers is seen to have been justified. Powers are the real potentialities which qualify minds and objects to participate in causal relationships. Turning aside now from arguments concerning the irreducibility of powers, I want to clarify one further aspect of this definition. The definition makes no distinction among causal conditions paralleling the distinction I have drawn between the first and third factors of this five-factor account of dispositional properties. It implies that all things must have specific powers in order to qualify as causal conditions, and, therefore, that the mind or object named as the first factor is on a par with the supplementary causal conditions of the third factor. This is as it should be, because all the members of a set of causal conditions are of equal importance in being. In every case in which something acts as a causal condition, there are innumerable minds and objects which could not have contributed to the production of the change which occurs. In order to account for the fact that this has been a causal condition, we are required to infer that it has or had a power which the others do not have.

Rather than there being a metaphysical justification, it

seems to me that there is a pragmatic excuse for distinguishing the first and third factors. This is evident in that portion of Hume's discussion of abstract ideas where the power of the mind to think of represented ideas is emphasized to the exclusion of any reference to powers which the sign and the need of reflection must also possess. Other men may think of the same determinate idea and feel the same intellectual need, but still fail to conceive of the relevant ideas, and Hume's problem is to tell us why some men are able to think of these ideas when circumstances require. There are a variety of these pragmatic reasons for our interest in one of a set of causal conditions; one cause may be the most difficult of a set of causal conditions to satisfy, or the condition which suffers the most spectacular change when the set is complete, or the cause which is least under control in circumstances where an undesirable reaction may be triggered. These and other practical reasons for our attending to one of a set of causal conditions are reflected in our habit of coining dispositional predicates for only a very small number of the causes contributing to the production of any change. Thus we say that a man is inclined to be nervous, but there are no comparable expressions for the pressures and irritations which frequently make him ill; and we do not coin phrases for these supplementary conditions until an attempt is made to cure the man by isolating and eliminating them.

There is good reason to doubt whether this practical interest should be an influence upon the organization of a metaphysical inquiry. However, so long as we recognize that supplementary causal conditions have powers, it makes no difference to this book whether we say that there are five, or only four, factors in the realist analysis of powers. In recognition of the pragmatic interest, I prefer to leave it at five, though I agree that ultimately there are only four categorically different factors: the causal conditions, the change they produce, the causal relationship which is constituted by the relation of these first two, and the real potentialities which qualify the relevant minds and objects to be causal conditions for the production of the change. This completes the *ad seriatim* explication of these factors.

I have been arguing that there is a crucial logical relation between the causal relationship and potentiality, and this has largely come out in the definition of powers. They are said to be the properties which qualify minds and objects for participation in causal relationships. Our understanding of this relation can be sharpened even more by way of a brief review of our conclusions. It has been said that causes produce effects dependent upon them for their occurrence; and also, that we can divide minds and objects into two classes, things of the kinds which produce a particular sort of effect, and things of those kinds which do not produce it. Furthermore, it has been said that we account for the fact that things of the former kinds do produce this change by inferring that they have real potentialities which qualify them to initiate or undergo the change. Now supposing that the arguments which support these claims are valid, it follows that the fact of having potentialities is *logically prior* to the fact of being a causal condition which contributes to the production of an effect.

The first consequence of this priority is that we can formulate a principle of argument which will be useful for the discussion of Chapter 2: Whenever there is causal sufficiency and necessity, we infer that the change produced is being effected by causal conditions which must have certain potentialities as a condition for producing it.

The other symptom of this logical relation is the characteristic openness of dispositional properties. If something is yellow, it will appear that way whenever anyone looks at it under natural light. There is no limit to the number of times that the test can be made. This may not seem to be a general rule; glass is said to be "fragile," but we cannot repeat a successful experiment which proves that it is. The example is beyond dispute, but it does not discredit the notion that powers are typically open. This notion applies to the behavior of kinds of things as well as to the histories of individual things. We say that whenever an object is of a certain kind, it has the potentiality common to things of that kind; under the circumstances, fulfillment of the supplementary conditions will invariably produce a certain change.

Finally, I want to consider two major difficulties in the realist theory of causal relationships and real potentialities. The first one is the need to account for the fact that a certain effect invariably occurs when a set of causal conditions is complete; this is a problem apart from any that we have discussed. The second difficulty is the need to elaborate the claim that objects and minds participate in causal relationships by virtue of having a potentiality; people will agree that the nature of potentiality remains obscure.

When Hume addresses himself to the first problem, he marvels that thought should be provided with an orderly stream of ideas. The mechanism of association is wholly mysterious to him, and he writes:

> To consider the matter aright, reason is nothing but a wonderful and unintelligible instinct in our souls, which carries us along a certain train of ideas, and endows them with particular qualities, according to their particular situations and relations. This instinct, 'tis true, arises from past observation and experience; but can any one give the ultimate reason, why past experience and observation produces such an effect any more than why nature alone shou'd produce it? Nature may certainly produce whatever can arise from habit: Nay, habit is nothing but one of the principles of nature, and derives all its force from that origin.[15]

In seeking an ultimate explanation of why prior experience of the conjunction of objects and present observation of one of them should force us to think of the other, Hume raises the fundamental issue in all analyses of causality: Why should it be that things produce just the effects they do produce? The fact that substances have powers is no help to us now, for part of the difficulty is to explain why things are empowered to behave as they do. Why is it that they are able to, and do act in certain ways when it is conceivable that their powers might have restricted them to different actions? None of the proposed solutions to this problem is convincing. Science provides ever more accurate descriptions of the world, but Hume would be likely to add, as scientists do, that their explanations only point to conjunctions more fundamental than the ones being explained. Short of a reference to divine purpose, we must some day come to elements whose causal relations can only be explained as invariant conjunctions. We shall still be able to say that the effect is produced by its causal conditions, and that it is dependent upon them; but we shall never know why this should be.

The second problem may be less intractable. There must be further discussion of the claim that causal relationships could not develop if the causal conditions did not have potentialities for participating in them. The nature of potentiality will have to be considered, and there will have to be an account of the relation between potentialities and those features of minds and objects which constitute their actuality. In the case of mental dispositions, we must determine the relation between the potentialities and the constituent factors of mind which I have described as nonintrospectable mental states. Similarly, discussion is required of the relation between the potentialities of physical objects and factors such as their shape, mass and molecular structure.

Though his discussion of abstract ideas leads to problems like these, Hume has nothing positive to say about them. Aristotle has quite a lot to say on these topics, however, and his conclusions will be the basis for discussion in Chapter 4. For the present, I want to suppose that this five-factor analysis of dispositional properties is coherent enough to stand criticism. In the last part of this chapter, and in the next chapter, there will be an analysis of some empiricist responses to the ideas of causal sufficiency and necessity, and real potentiality. Chapter 3 will be devoted to criticism, and elaboration, of the claim that the mind is partly constituted of what have been called "nonintrospectable mental states"; we recall that mind is supposed to owe its potentialities to these states.

Ic. *Re-examination of Hume's position;* 1] *Hume's attack on idea of causal necessity;* 2] *His objections to idea of power;* 3] *Criticism of his skeptical conclusions.*

In those passages for which Hume is most famous, there are reductive analyses of the ideas of both necessary connection (the distinction between causal sufficiency and necessity is collapsed in Hume's discussion), and potentiality. When writing of necessity, Hume argues as follows:

> Upon this head I repeat what I have often had occasion to observe, that as we have no idea, that is not deriv'd from an impression, we must find some impression, that gives rise to this idea of necessity, if we assert we have really such an idea. In order to do this I consider, in what objects necessity is commonly suppos'd to lie; and finding that it is always ascrib'd to causes and effects, I turn my eye to two objects supposed to be plac'd in that relation; and examine them in all the situations, of which they are susceptible. I immediately perceive, that they are contiguous in time and place, and that the object we call cause precedes the other we call effect. In no one instance can I go any farther, nor is it possible for me to discover any third relation betwixt these objects.[16]

Because there is no impression of a necessary connection, we are to conclude that there is no causal necessity. This is the core of the reductionist attack.

We could interpret Hume's remark conservatively, and assume that he means it to apply only to causal relations in the external world. This would be in keeping with such claims as that, ". . . after we have observ'd the resemblance (between two impressions or ideas) in a sufficient number of instances, we immediately feel a determination of the mind to pass from one object to its usual attendant, and to conceive it in a stronger light upon account of that relation."[17] In this passage and others, it is clear that Hume recognizes necessary causal relations in the sequence of our ideas. There are other places, however, where no concession is made to the claim that there are necessary connections, and in those passages, the admission that we "feel a determination of the mind" becomes the much more skeptical claim that the determination of the mind is just a feeling. In that event, there will be no necessary causal relations prescribing the order of events in either mind or the external world.

Someone might object that there are ideas of reason which are not mere copies of impressions, and that the idea of causal necessity is one of these, but Hume has, to his own satisfaction at least, already forestalled this objection. He claims to have established ". . . two very obvious principles" which justify the conclusion that there are no ideas of necessary causal relations. There is first the principle ". . . that Reason alone can never give rise to any original idea," and second, ". . . that Reason, as distinguished from experience, can never make us conclude, that cause or productive quality is absolutely requisite to every beginning of existence."[18]

With respect to the first principle; Reason can give rise to no new ideas because ". . . the operations of human understanding divide themselves into two kinds, the comparing of ideas and the inferring of matters of fact."[19] Reason compares ideas according to the seven philosophic relations: resemblance, identity, space and time, proportions of quantity, degrees of quality, contrariety, and cause and effect. The relation of cause and effect may also be used as a rule for making inferences. When objects or events have been observed in constant or regular conjunction, the impression or idea of one of them is sufficient to make us infer from it to the idea of the other. Overall, reason's activity, as Hume describes it, is very closely circumscribed. All the ideas that it compares or infers originate as impressions, or are constructed by the mind out of impressions. There are no impressions of necessary connection, therefore there is no idea of it.

The first principle is thought to establish that the idea of causal necessity could not be an idea of reason. This, if true, should be conclusive, but Hume goes farther. His second principle, quoted above is thought to be added proof that there cannot be such an idea. This principle is the conclusion of an argument which draws upon a number of Hume's assumptions. The argument runs as follows: There is no idea of a necessary connection between a set of causal conditions and their effect, and hence the causal conditions and effect are related only as conjuncts in space and time. They may be distinguished from one another, and therefore may be conceived separately. But notice, the conceivability of an idea is a proof of the possible existence of its object. Conception, after all, is merely the entertaining and relating of ideas, and ideas are copies of impressions, differing from them only for being less lively and forceful. Therefore, to say that what is thought might exist is only to say that our ideas might become more vivid and forceful than they are. There is only one consideration which could make us deny that something might possibly exist: a contradiction cannot exist. But neither can it be conceived, and we are here conceiving of an event without conceiving that other events have occurred antecedently to it. Consequently the claim that an event can exist without its having had antecedent causal conditions cannot be a contradiction. It is now established that the object of our conceiving could exist as we conceive of it. However paradoxical, reason cannot dispute this conclusion, because reason only compares ideas and makes inferences based on past observations of constant conjunctions. Reason will have to accept the claim that ". . . there is no absolute nor metaphysical necessity that every beginning of existence shou'd be attended with an object (a cause)."[20]

This is the argument, and we can reasonably ask why Hume has bothered to offer it, when he has already denied that causal necessity can be an idea of reason. The explanation, I suggest, is that he wants to undercut the assumptions which prompt rationalists to argue that there *must* be such an idea. Rationalists suppose that causal conditions produce their effects, that the effects are existentially dependent upon their antecedent causal conditions, and that an effect occurs because of the assembly of causal conditions which have potentialities qualifying them to bring it about. I would guess that Hume finds this battery of assumptions intolerable, believing as he does that rationalists can explain too much by making them. We are able to account for the constant conjunctions that are found in experience, and this absolves us from having to engage in the fruitless search after an empiricist justification for induction. If it is admitted that our explanations are compelling, then no one is likely to be satisfied when he is told that there is no impression of causal necessity, and there is likely to be a general demand that provision be made for ideas of reason. If this were to happen, Hume's strictures against admitting reason's free activity would be threatened, and along with them, all the rest of his empiricism.

Hume secures his position against this threat by arguing that the rationalists' purported explanation of constant conjunction is a delusion. The ideas of production and existential dependence are crucial to the rationalist explanation, and Hume sets out to demolish them. The way to do this is to argue that an effect is not tied to its antecedent causes by way of the relation of production and dependence. If the rationalist is correct, the cause must always come before the effect as a condition for the effect's occurrence. But it is *not* necessary that the cause should be antecedent, says Hume; look, we can imagine the one without the other. As conceivability is Hume's criterion for possible existence, it must be true that events can occur without there having been antecedent conditioning events. *This* is the vital point; and for the reason that if an event can exist independently of antecedent causal conditions, then surely it need not be produced by them, or be dependent upon them on those other occasions when its occurrence is subsequent to the gathering together of causal conditions. It is true that the events are customarily conjoined in our experience, but the rationalist has misinterpreted this fact as the sign of a peculiar bond between cause and effect. He has subsequently tried to capitalize on his original mistake by arguing that he can explain the constant conjunction by pointing to the reputed bond. The rationalist is in error; there is no bond, and there is no warrant for having to acknowledge a special rational faculty, and a rational idea of causal necessity.

This is a very daring argument. Because we can imagine a world in which there is no causal sufficiency and necessity, Hume would have us believe that there is none in our world, but this argument is certainly invalid: what we imagine that the world might have been is no account of what it is.

Let us suppose, however, that the idea of causal necessity is demolished. Under these circumstances, the idea of potentiality must also be rejected, and this for two reasons. First, Hume can apply his normal empiricist principles to determine whether there can be an idea of potentiality. He makes it very concise: "All ideas are deriv'd from, and represent impressions. We never have any impression, that contains any power or efficacy. We never therefore have any idea of power."[21] When a substance has performed a certain way on a number of occasions, we may suppose that it has a potentiality for effecting changes of this kind, but this explanation is said to be more popular than philosophical.[22] The second reason for dispensing with the idea of potentiality bears on the claim made in the last section that substances qualify to produce effects, because of having potentialities. If, however, the idea of production is dismissed, it is pointless to ascribe potentialities to things; minds and objects do not require powers for producing effects, if, in fact, they are not producing them. Thus, given Hume's empiricism, and the special principles which he applies in analyzing the notion of causal necessity, we are encouraged to surrender the idea of potentiality as we have already been deprived of the idea of necessary connection.

If we accept Hume's analysis of the ideas of potentiality and causal necessity, his discussion of abstract ideas will be a shambles. A single determinate idea could only represent other ideas if it (in conjunction with other relevant conditions) was sufficient for the thinking of the represented ideas. Now, however, Hume has argued that any kind of idea can follow upon completion of the set of causal conditions; there is no causal sufficiency and necessity to determine that some particular idea must always follow. Under the circumstances, it is no longer reasonable to say that a single, determinate idea represented the ideas that succeed it in thought. Hume now implies that there is no special connection between the one and those others.

Without going back to reformulate his views on abstract ideas, Hume draws some general conclusions about the nature of mind. He describes it as ". . . nothing but a heap or collection of different perceptions, united together by certain relations."[23] Unfortunately, this mind could not function as ours really do, because it is deprived of the faculties required to make experience coherent. According to Hume's more constructive passages, the coherence of thought depends upon the mechanism of association, and association in turn is accounted for by way of a dispositional theory of memory: memory is the set of powers which enable mind to participate in the causal relationships where circumstances prompt the mind to recognize objects and events, and to recall the ideas of things which have been frequently conjoined with these objects and events in the past. Hume endorses this theory by his every reference to the habits or powers which must be acquired to promote the association of our ideas, but now he has denied that there are powers, and he has failed to provide in any other way for the recall of an image that has been constantly conjoined with another which is presently being thought or perceived.

This has important repercussions for the kind of thinking that the mind can perform. It entails, for example, that there can be no schematized trains of thought which extend in time beyond the limits of the specious present. Music will be neither composed nor heard, because there will be no comprehension of the musical forms which determine the sequences of the notes. An ordered series of notes will be utterly unintelligible to a mind unable to mark every successive note as the melodic consequent of those that have gone before, and unable to anticipate the proper or likely development of the melodic line. When Hume writes about the association of ideas, he makes clear how important it is for the mind to be applying a conceptual schema like a musical form. Indeed, his remarks on this point are similar to Kant's discussion of the synthesis of reproduction. Without this synthesis, thought cannot be coherent over any period longer than the specious present. Having eliminated memory, Hume will be describing a mind which performs all its operations within that span. This mind is not even a heap. It would be more truly described as a series of very thin slices.

Hume's reductionist principles cannot be seriously intended for application to mind, because if they are, they entail such a falsification of what we know of mind as to provide a reductio ad absurdum of the premises. In fact, there is every reason to believe that Hume's skepticism about mind is not very genuine. There are occasional gestures like the passage quoted above, but for the most part Hume is firm that ideas are necessarily connected in thought and that the mind's possession of habits conditions their association.

Though we may save Hume's analysis of mind by construing it in terms of realist conceptions, it would be mistaken to say that Hume fails to apply reductionist arguments in his description of the natural world. He does apply them, and the consequences of his skepticism are admirably summed up by Hegel:

Touching this principle it has been justly observed that in what we call Experience, as distinct from mere single perception of single facts, there are two elements. The one is the matter, infinite in its multiplicity, and as it stands a mere set of singulars: the other is the form, the characteristics of universality and necessity. Mere experience no doubt offers many, perhaps innumerable cases of similar perceptions: but, after all, no multitude, however great, can be the same thing as universality. Similarly, experience affords perceptions of changes succeeding each other and of objects in juxtaposition: but it presents no necessary connexion. If perception, therefore is to maintain its claim to be the sole basis of what

men hold for truth, universality and necessity appear
something illegitimate: they become an accident of our
mind, a mere custom, the content of which might be
otherwise than it is.[24]

The necessary connection to which Hegel refers is of course
the causal sufficiency and necessity for which I have argued
above. His reference to universality is an implicit reference
to potentiality by way of the openness which is a consequence
of the relation between causal sufficiency and necessity, and
potentiality: minds and objects of certain kinds will have
potentialities which qualify them to contribute to the production of a specific change and the change will occur *whenever* supplementary conditions are fulfilled. This is the
universality which is not exhausted by any multitude of occurrences.

Because he criticizes Hume's analysis for entailing that
experience might be other than it is, Hegel might be con-
strued as denying that the world could ever suffer the radical
upset of its causal laws, but to the contrary, I think Hegel
would admit that alternative world-orders are conceivable,
and that the world revealed in everyday experience might
eventually come to be like some imagined universe. A different point is at issue. Whatever changes it may some day
undergo, the world has certain formal characteristics now.
When he remarks that on Hume's theory the world might
be other than as it is, Hegel is pointing out the discrepancy
between the world as it is at present and as it ought to be if
Hume's account were true.

Hegel argues — and I agree — that the world has been
misdescribed, or perhaps just underdescribed. Hume has
failed to discern the causal sufficiency and necessity, and the
potentialities which are conditions for the order which exists
in the world. In order to establish once more that these are
factors in the world, let us imagine two states of affairs; first,
a world that has no causal sufficiency and necessity in it, and,
second, a world devoid of powers.

In the first instance, all causal relations will be merely
spatial and temporal relations. At one point, Hume describes

the characteristic features of these relations. We are told that, ". . . the relations of contiguity and distance betwixt two objects may be chang'd merely by an alternation of their place without any change in the objects themselves or their ideas."[25] This passage is one of several in which Hume reveals that he conceives of things related in space and time as atoms of a sort, and, consequently, that he believes that we can change the spatial and temporal positions of a thing without modifying its properties or those of the things to which it is spatially and temporally related. Given this view, we should be able to infer the converse of the statement quoted above: just as the positions of things can be changed without that modifying their qualities, so it should be possible for them to suffer changes in quality without that making a difference to their relative positions. Thus it makes no difference to the properties of the pieces of furniture in a room if we rearrange them, and, similarly, the cabinets and lamps are unmodified if the piano is tuned.

It is well to remember at this point that the claims being made about relations of things in space and time apply to relations of cause and effect. Hume has defined a cause as an "object precedent and contiguous to another, and where all the objects resembling the former are plac'd in like relations of precedency and contiguity to those objects, that resemble the latter."[26] This is to say that the relation of cause and effect is no more than the relation of precedence and contiguity, and it invites the application of the two principles which have just been seen to apply to things that are conceived as mere conjuncts in space and time. Consider the example of an explosion. According to the first principle described above, the dynamite will explode if the heat source is applied directly to it, or is held a thousand miles away. Applying the converse, we should expect the dynamite to explode whether we put a match to its fuse, or merely look at it. Generally, it would appear that objects may fall into and out of conjunctions in space and time, read cause and effect relations, without any effect on themselves or their sometime relata.

It will be said that this is a distortion of Hume's theory, but I suggest to the contrary that it follows immediately from Hume's principles, and, moreover, that he affirms that it does. Hume writes:

> According to the precedent doctrine, there are no objects, which by mere survey, without consulting experience, we can determine to be the cause of any other; and no objects, which we can certainly determine in the same manner not to be causes. Anything can produce any thing. Creation, annihilation, motion, reason, volition; all these may arise from one another, or from any other object we can imagine. Nor will this appear strange, if we compare two principles explain'd above, that the constant conjunction of objects determines their causation, and that properly speaking, no objects are contrary to each other, but existence and nonexistence. Where objects are not contrary, nothing hinders them from having that constant conjunction, on which the relation of cause and effect totally depends.[27]

Hume does recognize that only a small portion of all possible conjunctions are discovered in experience, yet there is no difference in principle between these and the unexperienced, but possible combinations. In every possible relationship, experienced or otherwise, things related will be nothing more than accidental conjuncts in space and time.

We can draw either one of two logical conclusions from Hume's principles. On the one hand, effects are most unlikely to be constantly conjoined to antecedent causal conditions if their only relation is a temporal one. Anything can, and indeed should, follow upon anything else. There should be utter chaos in the world. The alternative and logically prior, entailment is that no effect should ever occur for want of a sufficient condition to produce it. In either event, Hume's principles entail a world to which the mind he describes could never become adjusted. There would be no recurrent patterns in this world, and mind, failing to perceive constant conjunctions, would never acquire its habits of association. No idea or impression would prompt us to think of any other, and experience would either be an endless fairy tale as causal conditions produced an unpredictable variety of effects, or, on the assumption of a causal theory of perception (and supposing that causes were not sufficient to produce effects), a total blank. All this for want of causal necessity.

An empiricist whose confidence in Hume is still unshaken is not likely to be impressed by one more *reductio,* but at the risk of belaboring the point, I should say that the implication of the hypothesis that there are no powers reinforces the second possible implication of the claim that there is no causal necessity. The absence of powers entails that there are no things disposed to cause or suffer effects, and consequently, no group of substances should constitute a set of causal conditions, and no mind or object should ever suffer the modification of any of its properties.

These various entailments make it clear that Hume's metaphysics is tailored to describe imaginary worlds having no significant likeness to our own. This result frustrates the aims of a science which normally purports to describe the categorical features of the real world, and we might want to reject his metaphysics on this ground alone. But no question remains when Hume argues that his conclusions do have some bearing upon our world. There is no choice now but to dismiss his skeptical empiricism as an example of those philosophies which are plainly misconceived.

2

COUNTERFACTUAL CONDITIONALS

Contemporary logical empiricists are unreconstructed Humeans, and their adaptation of Hume's principles must be considered before it is said categorically that reductionist empiricism is unable to afford a satisfactory metaphysics.

Logical empiricists are perhaps best described as philosophers who extract the formal elements other than spatial and temporal relations from processes in the world, discover those elements or versions of them in language, and then argue that the original extraction was justified, because the world can do without its formal elements so long as language has them. Treatment of the formal elements follows an established procedure: Nothing of which we have no impression can have being in the world; because we cannot see or touch them, it will follow that causal sufficiency and necessity, and potentiality cannot be real. Obviously, however, these are notions which have an important function in our descriptions of the world, and the next step in the empiricist argument must prove that there are counterparts for these elements in certain features of language. Causal sufficiency and necessity are provided for, as subsequent discussion will show, by describing the relation of premises and consequent in a formal language system, and potentiality is said to be a nuance expressed when terms like "can" and "able" are used in ordinary speech.

There ought to be a criterion for the success of reductionist linguistic analyses of this kind, and a likely one is the requirement that linguistic solutions must eliminate the difficulties which project us into metaphysical discussions. The object of this chapter is to determine whether this requirement is satisfied when logical empiricists give their analyses of potentiality and the causal relationship. For purposes of exposition, it will help to begin with a survey of their discussion of potentiality. This will carry us to their analysis of causal relationships, and, finally, back again to the notion of potentiality.

IIa. Survey of the problem; 1] View that dispositions are to be analyzed by reference to causal-law statements; 2] Difficulty: rules of material implication do not enable us to distinguish true causal-law statements from certain other counterfactuals.

Nelson Goodman discusses the considerations which direct a logical empiricist account of dispositional properties, and at one point, he makes this observation:

> The peculiarity of dispositional predicates is that they seem to be applied to things in virtue of possible rather than actual occurrences — and possible occurrences are for us no more admissible as unexplained elements than are occult capacities. The problem, then, is to explain how dispositional predicates can be assigned to things solely on the basis of actual occurrences — that is, in terms of manifest predicates — for the correct assignment of dispositional predicates to things.[1]

Hume made this same point when he prescribed that all our ideas of the world must copy impressions of it. In its modern guise, Hume's rule is the verificationist principle that a statement about the world can only be true, and hence meaningful, if we can imagine the observable difference that its truth would make to our experience. If we accept this principle, it will have to be admitted that Hume and Goodman are correct; the reality of dispositional properties will not make an immediate difference to our perceptions. There are no perceptions of real potentiality, and, therefore, it will not be true, or even intelligible, to say that dispositional properties ought to be described as real potentialities. Some alternative analysis of powers will have to be considered.

Arthur Pap offers an explicit statement of the view that empiricists usually adopt:

> To ascribe dispositions to a thing which exist even while they are not displayed, is not to ascribe to it any metaphysical, hidden powers. It merely amounts to the assertion that a law, expressed as a subjunctive conditional, is true even though the conditions it refers to are not always realized. To say that a girl, at this moment cold and reserved, has the disposition to be amorous, is to say that she would be amorous if she were exposed to the appropriate stimuli.[2]

In outline, this is the theory that talk about dispositions is to be understood through the analysis of conditional, "if-then," statements. We recognize it as the second version of the causal law analysis of powers. Gilbert Ryle helped to popularize this theory when he argued that dispositions, powers and capacities are merely "inference tickets"; given the information that a set of causal conditions has been or will be satisfied, we infer that a particular change did, or will, occur.[3]

The argument which terminates in this conclusion develops in two stages; dispositional properties are analyzed by way of reference to causal laws, and the causal laws are reduced in status to causal law statements. The first move in the first stage comes when we accept the principle that nothing can have reality in the world, unless we can perceive it. Because dispositional properties are not the sorts of things which can be observed, we must suppose that they are not real properties, and a reductionist account of them is now in order. Pap takes the next step, just quoted, when he moves the focus of the analysis from being to language; he talks of "dispositional predicates" rather than of dispositional properties. It is not enough, however, merely to suppose that dispositions are linguistic expressions. Two considerations require that we provide something more. First, statements with dispositional predicates, together with "can" and "could have" statements, might be regarded as implicit assertions that dispositions are real properties possessed by things in the world, and something must be done to discourage this inference. Second, if dispositions are not properties of things, there has to be a discussion of how it can be the case that some things, rather than others, qualify to suffer and effect specific changes; if it is not the possession of a dispositional property which qualifies the causal conditions and distinguishes them from other things, what does? The solution to both of these difficulties is to argue, as Pap does, that statements having dispositional predicates, or "can" or "could have" as their verbs, should be analyzed as counterfactual conditionals which express causal laws.

I have already discussed some of the features of this causal-law analysis. The principal notion is that being disposed to contribute to the production of a change is identical with being a mind or object which falls within the determination of a causal law. When we ascribe a power to something, we are only claiming, it is said, that this thing will act as the law determines when supplementary conditions are fulfilled. Two other aspects of the problem are taken in stride. There is recognition that some dispositions are apparently peculiar to individuals. "If-then" statements describing the behavior of these individuals cannot express causal laws, because the statements do not have universal scope, but these statements are assimilated to the causal law analysis by supposing that science will eventually discover laws having universal scope which will cover the behavior described by the statements. The openness which we attribute to powers is the other aspect to be considered, and this is made out to be a consequence of the universal scope of causal laws; the laws determine that a change will occur *whenever* appropriate causal conditions are assembled.

In the second stage of their argument, logical empiricists apply the same demand to the notion of causal laws as was made in the analysis of powers; they argue that a statement purporting to describe or refer to some matter of fact in the world cannot be true or false, and meaningful, unless we can imagine the observable states of affairs which would make the statement true or false. This means that it is only significant to claim that there are causal laws operative in the world if we can imagine what it would be like to perceive these laws.

It would seem that the realist theory of causal laws could easily withstand this test; for after all, there is nothing radical about the claim that there are limitations in nature such that things of certain kinds will naturally interact to produce some effect. Obvious as this is to some of us, it is anathema to orthodox Humeans. Hume has insisted that, in principle, anything can cause anything, and he has succeeded in reducing all causal relationships to accidental, however constant, conjunctions. The world he describes is one in which there is no provision for kinds and limits. Remember now that the logical empiricist is a Humean and an atomist: hard as he may look, he sees nothing but particulars that are isolated from one another by space and time. He certainly does not see kinds or limitations, and if this is what the causal law realist would have him look for, the statement that there are real causal laws must be unintelligible to him.

This theory of real causal laws is so much in conflict with Humean assumptions, that verificationists rarely consider it. For the most part, they devote their critical analysis to the idea that real causal laws might be identical with the sum of causal relationships in which a particular set of causal conditions produces a certain effect. This is the notion that the law determining that water shall boil is identical with the set of occasions when heat has been applied and water has boiled. This is an initially promising alternative for the verificationists, because each of the causal relationships in a set will be an observable event, but it is nonetheless unacceptable on the grounds that causal laws have universal scope, and no sum of particular occurrences will ever exhaust their universality. We could never imagine all of the possible members of a set of causal relationships, and, having equated the reality of causal laws with this set, verificationists argue that there is no possibility of confirming the claim that causal laws are real.

There was a time when this conclusion had serious repercussions for empiricist thought. It was said that causal law statements do not refer to or describe an occurrent matter of fact; but, also, that failure to satisfy the verifiability principle entails that causal-law statements have no cognitive value. This was one of Ludwig Wittgenstein's ideas, and, given the assumption that statements are only meaningful if there is a possibility that they may be confirmed, his conclusion does follow. But as it happened, most empiricists had no taste for the radical claim that scientists are talking nonsense, and, sacrificing their verificationist assumptions, they allowed that causal law statements are meaningful, even though causal laws are not observable and therefore cannot be real.[4]

This is the present-day attitude, and it invites a reductionist solution to the problem of causal laws. They must be provided for in a way that will not conflict with the view that there is no reality to factors which are unobservable, and this is done by saying that causal laws are merely conditional, "if-then," statements.

Empiricists believe that they lose none of the cogency of their analysis of powers when they subsequently give this reductionist account of causal laws, and, indeed, they see a very appreciable advantage in the fact that they can now give a simple logical interpretation of the openness which is claimed for dispositions. The situation is this: The indeterminacy of a power with respect to the time and place of its realization has been identified with the universal scope of causal laws, and is understood as the fact that an effect will occur whenever a set of causal conditions is assembled. The reduction of causal laws to conditional statements, now enables us to see that this analysis is the enthymematic version of an inference. The causal law statement is a suppressed major premise which says that if a set of causal conditions are fulfilled an effect will accrue. Adding the minor premise that here are instances of all the causal conditions of the set, we infer that the effect must occur now. Consequently, saying that an effect will occur whenever causal conditions are satisfied only means that we can deduce the consequent of a causal law statement, as often as we have a minor premise saying that the causal conditions described in the antecedent of the major premise are assembled. It is their success in giving this simple logical twist to the analysis which buoys empiricists' confidence in their theory of dispositions.

We know that absolute confidence in this theory cannot be justified, because it is the view which Austin has criticized as the "shall-if" analysis of "can" statements. Austin reminds us that this reductionist proposal equates being able to do something with the fact of doing it when supplementary causal conditions are satisfied. This means that things do not have powers when conditions are not fulfilled and they are not suffering or initiating a change. If we accept the common-sense view that is built into ordinary language, we can simply reject this counterfactual-conditional analysis. That, however, would be dangerous. The logical empiricist analysis is supported by a highly regarded theory of knowledge, and it would be foolish to neglect a development of that theory in preference to uncritical popular opinion. It may be the case that ordinary language and thought are mistaken, and that a man does not have an ability, when he is not performing. With that possibility in mind, the remainder of this chapter will aim to determine whether the empiricists have successfully demonstrated that the implications of the common-sense view are in fact misguided.

A major difficulty in their analysis is close at hand. The statement "Porcelain shatters when dropped" is true even if no one ever drops a plate. According to the rules of material implication, a counterfactual is true if its antecedent is false. This is satisfactory, because we want the statement to be true even though no test is being made, but there is a problem in distinguishing this true causal law statement from several other kinds of counterfactual statements. Consider these examples: "If you flapped your arms, you would fly," "Asbestos melts when exposed to fire," and "My luck is always good when I wear a charm." The first counterfactual describes a fanciful coupling of events; the second purports to be a causal law, but is not; and the third describes an accidental, though possibly constant, conjunction of events. If we indiscriminately apply the rules of material implication, there will be occasions when each of these three examples will be logically indistinguishable from the true causal law statement, "Porcelain shatters when dropped"; the antecedents of all four may be false when uttered, and the statements will then be true.

What we require are special logical rules for distinguishing true causal law statements from the other counterfactuals. One way to make the distinction is to introduce the notion of causal implication, but this would be objectionable to logical empiricists, because it would violate their Humean convictions. Another method is to say that true causal-law statements are analytic, but this too is rejected, because it would require elaborate restatement of a conditional to make it analytically true, and because empiricists do not believe that causal relations are analytic.

IIb. Two attempts to solve problem; 1] First attempts: Carnap's reduction-sentences; (a) Reduction-sentences described; (b) The advantages of this method of distinguishing among counterfactuals; (c) Do reduction-sentences eliminate dispositional predicates? i. Why these predicates cannot be eliminated in this way; ii. Carnap: string of reduction-sentences as a definition of dispositional predicate; iii. Four replies to Carnap; (d) Carnap's attempt to distinguish among counterfactuals rejected.

Among the other alternatives open to us are two particularly influential analyses. They are respectively Rudolf Carnap's method of "reduction sentences," and R. B. Braithwaite's view that true causal-law statements are those which have been or can be deduced from higher-level hypotheses of an established scientific system. In spite of the fact that there are other important contributions, notably Goodman's, I have concentrated upon these two, believing that I can best establish the salient issues here by doing so.

Despite some other changes in his thinking, Carnap continues to regard the notion of reduction sentences well enough to have endorsed it, without major change, in a recent paper.[5] He also mentions in this paper that he expects to explain, in the not-too-distant future, a new logical technique for introducing dispositional predicates. However, until that further statement of his is published, I think we must regard the description of reduction sentences as Carnap's definitive view on the subject of dispositional predicates.

A reduction sentence has the form:

$$\text{If } Q_1, \text{ then, if } Q_2 \text{ then } Q_3$$

Q_1 refers to a set of test conditions; Q_2 characterizes the test effect; Q_3 is the dispositional predicate that may be ascribed when the test conditions are fulfilled and the effect results. Carnap stipulates that the sentence must have valid arguments for Q_1 and Q_2. This means that Q_1 and Q_2, which are simple statements, must be true. A sentence lacking valid arguments for these two ". . . would not tell us anything about how to use the predicate 'Q_3' and therefore could not be taken as a reduction sentence."[6] Carnap slightly exaggerates to make his point. Of course we would know how to use such a dispositional predicate as "can fly" in talking of a human being. The point is that we would never be justified in using it if we did not have observational evidence that he could perform in this way.

Reduction sentences are used in pairs. Coupled with the sentence which tells us when to ascribe Q_3 is a sentence prescribing a test for determining when Q_3 may not be predicated of something. This other sentence has the form:

$$\text{If } Q_4 \text{, then, if } Q_5 \text{ then } - Q_3$$

It tells us that a dispositional predicate cannot be ascribed, if a set of test conditions are assembled and a certain change results. This time, Carnap requires valid arguments for Q_4 and Q_5.

Together, the confirming or positive, and disconfirming or negative, reduction sentences constitute a "reduction pair." We are to operate with them in tandem in order to determine the applicability of a dispositional predicate. We wish, for example, to determine someone's taste in music. Positively, we say that if we show him a piano and he amuses himself by playing Mozart sonatas, then, yes, he is musically inclined and has leanings toward the classical period. The results of this test readily suggest a negative counterpart. We take him to hear a *musica viva* session of Stockhausen tapes, and he leaves at the intermission. His taste is rather more narrowly defined now, and we know better what dispositional predicate can be ascribed to him.

It does not follow, however, that failure to obtain the test effect of a positive reduction sentence means that the disposition is not present, and like failure with the effect described by the negative reduction sentence does not indicate that the property is present. Thus, if our man does not play Mozart or anything else when we point out a piano, it does not follow that he is not a musician with classical interests; he might only be shy or out of the mood. Similarly, he might listen intently to what he hears in a recital of advanced music, but that need not mean that he appreciates it. Perhaps this is his first exposure, and he is appalled. Not playing the piano and not walking out are not conclusive evidence for determining whether the dispositional predicate should be ascribed. We can only hope that repeated tests of these kinds will make it more or less likely that the predicate fits.

This is never completely satisfactory, because someone might have a disposition that evades all our tests for it. And therefore we require a "bilateral reduction sentence" to assure that the test effect determines whether the predicate should be attributed to something or not. The bilateral reduction sentence is a combination of an unusual reduction pair. It is a pair in which the terms referring to the test conditions, Q_1 and Q_4 are the same, and where the term characterizing the test effect Q_5 is the same as $-Q_2$. The statement form of a bilateral reduction sentence is:

If Q_1, then Q_3 if and only if Q_2

To distinguish true causal laws from the bogus counterfactuals, Carnap again makes a stipulation: there must be a valid argument for Q_1.

At first glance, this appears to be a less rigorous stipulation than was made for the positive and negative reduction sentences. For each of them, Carnap rules that both the causal conditions term, Q_1 and Q_4, and the test effect term, Q_2 and Q_5, must have valid arguments. In the case of the bilateral reduction sentence the only convention is that Q_1 must be true, but this is a sign of more rigor rather than less. The bilateral reduction sentence plays upon a tautology. It says: Given a valid argument for Q_1, then, either Q_2 or $-Q_2$. This is just a first step. In itself, this tautology would not be enough to make the bilateral reduction sentence so strong. The man who was shown a piano also had to choose between playing or not playing, but this was not a definitive test, because only half of it, his playing, indicated that he had the disposition. Not playing was not to be regarded as evidence one way or another.

In order to make this into the definitive test for a bilateral reduction sentence, we would have to develop the simple positive, or negative, reduction sentence in two ways. These are: 1] There must be a single pair of mutually exclusive test effects which exhaust the field of possible test effects in a particular context. In this event, nonoccurrence of the one test effect will entail the occurrence of the other one. 2] The set of test effects must be correlated with dispositional predicates which mutually exclude one another and which exhaust a field. The observation of one test effect will then be all the reason that can be required for ascribing one predicate: appearance of the second test effect will justify ascription of the other predicate.

We can imagine a situation in which half of a population of robots was constructed so that the presence of a piano was always a cue to sit down and play. If the other robots were equipped to do nothing but pluck banjos, this would be the basis for converting the positive reduction sentence mentioned above into a bilateral reduction sentence. The litmus test in chemistry is a more natural example, however. Let us suppose that there is no middle range of neutral solutions in which litmus does not change color. In that case, the paper turns either blue or pink. Not turning pink entails that the paper has turned blue. To these exclusive and exhaustive alternatives, we correlate exclusive dispositional predicates that exhaust the possible alternatives. A solution that turns litmus blue, we recall, is basic, and one that turns it pink is acidic. On these terms, the color of the paper when dipped into a solution definitively settles what predicate ought to be ascribed to the solution. Failure to observe the positive test effect, blue litmus paper, will not mean that the solution might still be basic; the litmus will have turned pink, and that means that the solution is not basic, but acidic. The dispositional predicates, acidic and basic, have been so correlated with the test effects, pink and blue, that the question of which dispositional predicate to assign is decided whenever we provide a valid argument for Q_1 by dropping the litmus into a solution.

Because of its stipulations, the notion of reduction sentences does permit us to distinguish true causal law statements from other counterfactuals. The reason for this is that causal-law statements are the only counterfactuals which can have all the required valid arguments; effects will always occur when causal conditions are satisfied. Fanciful counterfactuals and false causal-law statements are a different breed; the effects described by their consequents do not occur when the conditions described in the antecedents are fulfilled.

This solution to the problem becomes a bit strained only when we turn to the counterfactuals which describe accidental, but constant, conjunctions. There appear to be times when we do have the required valid arguments for both the antecedent and consequent of these conditional, and normally counterfactual, statements. Suppose that someone always experiences a personally favorable turning of events when he wears a charm: does this coupling of events justify our saying that it is his nature to be lucky? We answer that there is probably no cause to ascribe the dispositional predicate in question, because we believe that this is an accidental conjunction, and that either of the conjuncts can occur when the other does not. If we are right, and the conjunction is accidental, we should be able to arrange an experiment proving the independence of the conjuncts. In the event that our experiment is successful, the positive reduction sentence will lack one of its arguments: either the purported causal conditions will occur and the reputed effect will not, or the initial conditions will not be satisfied, and the man's luck will remain as good as before. Failure to satisfy both of the stipulations made for the reduction sentence will mean that we cannot ascribe the predicate "lucky," and this will justify the conclusion that the counterfactual is not a causal-law statement. The great drawback is that there are times, as in the case of the binary star example suggested in the first chapter, when there are no experiments which will help us to identify accidental constant conjunctions. Conjunctions like these, and the conditionals which describe them, pose a difficulty which will have to be reconsidered. But in spite of this, I want to assume that the notion of reduction sentences does satisfactorily distinguish true causal-law statements from the variety of other counterfactuals.

There is one minor difficulty which should also be mentioned. Consider the statement, "His yield would be higher if he would rotate crops more often." It is too late this year to make the test, but we have a law that covers the growth factor of seed like that which has been badly used. Though the present statement cannot have valid arguments, the law statement has had valid arguments in the past, and we therefore accept it as establishing the truth of the untestable statement.

Carnap's stipulations only provoke major worries when we recall their theoretical setting. Pap has written:

> To ascribe dispositions to a thing which exist even while they are not displayed, is not to ascribe to it any metaphysical, hidden powers. It *merely amounts* to the assertion that a law, expressed as a subjunctive conditional is true even though the conditions it refers to are not always realized.[7]

I have added italics to the phrase which makes it clear that Pap has the total elimination of dispositional predicates in mind. The motive, we recall, for dispensing with them is that unanalyzed dispositional predicates apparently attribute a potentiality to a mind or object; we say that a man has a quick temper and mean that he has the potentiality for turning to a rage on short notice, and over minor inconvenience. Logical empiricists analyze this statement into a counterfactual in order to show that the potentiality is really no more than a nuance of language. And now, after these pains have been taken, Carnap's reduction sentences subvert the program by reintroducing dispositional predicates as fixtures in the language. This at least appears to be the unavoidable consequence of what Carnap has to say about reduction sentences.

Carnap, himself, is not always clear about what *ought* to be said about the eliminability of dispositional predicates. He sometimes argues that dispositional predicates are not eliminable from reduction sentences, but he also suggests the circumstances in which they would be eliminable. Let us take up his arguments for the eliminability and ineliminability of these predicates, in that order.

Dispositional predicates can only be eliminated in favor of, or explicitly defined by, conditionals which describe causal conditions and effects, if the substitution of conditionals for dispositional predicates never changes the truth value of statements in which those predicates occur. This requirement is not satisfied when we attempt to replace dispositional predicates with conditionals which satisfy the stipulations which Carnap makes for his reduction sentences. For example, we can transform the true but at present untested statement, "This window opens" into a conditional reading, "If you clutch the handles and pull, this window will rise on its tracks." If we adopt Carnap's theory of reduction sentences, we can only ascribe the predicate "can open" in talking of this window, if there are valid arguments for the antecedent and consequent of the conditional. The ascription of the dispositional predicate is unwarranted in their absence, and the statement, "This window opens" will consequently be inappropriate if it is untested. This is to say that attempts to define dispositional predicates by way of reduction sentences will disqualify every claim about the world whose truth is not now being tested. Carnap recognizes that we regularly use dispositional language in circumstances where no test is made to justify the usage, and for this reason he denies that dispositional predicates can be eliminated in favor of conditionals with valid arguments.[8]

Indeed, there is a mistaken interpretation of their function in attempts to herald reduction sentences as a method for eliminating dispositional predicates. Reduction sentences only describe the conditions which must be satisfied if we are justifiably to assert that someone or something has a dispositional property. They are reports of verification procedures, and the tests they describe have a beginning and an end. We recognize that there is a difference between a test, and the property for whose existence we are testing; and acknowledging this distinction, we are not compelled to say that the thing tested ceases to have the dispositional property when the test ends. Correlatively, the dispositional predicate which we assign to things having the dispositional property will not be defined by, nor eliminated in favor of, terms which appear in the antecedents and consequents of reduction sentences. These terms only refer to observables, and they are no substitutes for the dispositional predicates which the theory of reduction sentences recognizes as primitives of the language.[9]

A formulation that makes dispositional predicates ineliminable must be unsatisfactory in the view of empiricists, and this evidently distresses Carnap, for in his recent paper he argues: "When both S (stimulus or causal conditions) and R (response or effect) are specified, then the disposition concept D_{sr} is thereby completely characterized in its meaning."[10] There is also a passage in *Testability and Meaning* in which Carnap describes the circumstances in which dispositional predicates can be eliminated. He writes:

> A set of reduction pairs is a partial determination of meaning only and can therefore not be replaced by a definition. Only if we reach, by adding more and more reduction pairs, a stage in which all cases are determined, may we go over to the form of a definition.[11]

As I understand it, this supposes a time when we will have test sentences permitting us to determine whether a member of any class of cases has a particular dispositional property. At this point, Carnap says, we may define the dispositional predicate by reference to the tests described in the various reduction sentences.

In fact, Carnap now argues that it has merely been a pragmatic interest which has prohibited us from regarding a single reduction pair as an explicit definition of a dispositional predicate. He explains as follows:

> The scientist wishes neither to determine all the cases of the third class (those in which we do not yet know whether or not a dispositional predicate should be ascribed) positively, nor all of them negatively, he wishes to leave these questions open until the results of further investigations suggest the statement of a new reduction pair: thereby some of the cases so far undetermined become determined positively and some negatively. If we now were to state a definition, we should have to revoke it at such a new state of the development of science and to state a new definition, incompatible with

the first one. If, on the other hand, we were now to state a reduction pair, we should merely have to add one or more reduction pairs at the new stage; and these pairs will be compatible with the first one. In this latter case we do not correct the determinations laid down in the previous stage but simply supplement them.[12]

It seems to me that Carnap has lost hold of the relevant distinction between observational and dispositional predicates; and that his proposal to use the former, in a string of reduction sentences, to define the latter, is open to numerous objections.

1] How could one know *a priori* that he had exhausted all the classes of cases to which a particular dispositional predicate might be ascribed? Presumably, he would have to know this, if he were to stop at some point and say that the string of reduction pairs used so far constitutes a definition of the predicate. Carnap does anticipate, in the quotation before the last one, that all classes of cases will have been investigated; but, again, how could one know this?

2] Carnap writes: "If a property or physical magnitude can be determined by different methods then we may state one reduction pair or one bilateral reduction sentence for each method."[13] This raises two sub-questions: (a) Would the definition include all the reduction pairs used for ascribing the predicate in this class of cases, or just one of the pairs? (b) If, as seems reasonable, we are to include all of them, how could we ever know that we had discovered all the possible methods which could justify the ascription of the dispositional predicate in this class of cases? Together with the first objection, these rather minor ones suggest that there would never be a time when we could be certain that we had exhausted either all classes of cases, or all methods of testing in any particular class of cases. The conclusion is that there would never be a time when we could establish the definition of a dispositional predicate by reference to a string of reduction sentences.

3]   Carnap supposes that scientists use reduction pairs to test one or more instances of a class, and that, determining whether or not a dispositional predicate may be attributed in these instances, they generalize their findings to cover the class. If Carnap is now taken literally, however, these generalizations will not be part of the definition. He says that the definition will consist of the set of reduction sentences, but reduction sentences only report that a dispositional predicate can be ascribed to an object on a certain occasion, because it responded in a certain way when tested. Under the circumstances, the proposed definition of the dispositional predicate will only describe a number of experiments; it will tell us how a number of particular things *have responded*, rather than how all things of these kinds *would respond*. Carnap cannot intend to leave himself open to this objection, first, because he is interested in particular observations as evidence for causal-law statements, and, second, because the suggested method for eliminating dispositional predicates conflicts with his remarks about the impossibility of using reduction sentences as explicit definitions of dispositional predicates. We must take Carnap to mean that the definitions of these predicates will consist of the law-statements which are generalized on the basis of observations reported by the various reduction sentences.

4]   This amended formulation is still ambiguous. The proposed definition will now consist of a set of law-statements, each of which has been generalized from reduction sentences which describe a certain kind of experiment conducted on the members of a certain class of cases. It is at least possible, however, that there might be different causal conditions producing different effects in every one of the classes of cases that are tested for the dispositional property. It is even possible, as suggested above, that there could be several different tests for the same property within a single class of cases. The set of law-statements which comprises the definition will consequently describe a wide variety of causal conditions and effects. Now it is wholly out of keeping with the idea of reduction sentences to suppose that this set could be the definition of a single dispositional predicate. Reduction sentences have been introduced in order to state the conditions under which it is justified to ascribe dispositional predicates, and it is said that a particular predicate is only legitimately ascribed when there are valid arguments for the antecedent and consequent of a specific reduction pair. These stipulations tie a dispositional predicate to certain observational predicates which describe relevant causes and effects. Though the predicate is not explictly definable in terms of these observational predicates, it is only identifiable by way of them. This is the original view, and if it is taken as definitive, no collection of law-statements describing various causal conditions and effects, can define a single dispositional predicate. Rather, there will be as many dispositional predicates as there are different law-statements generalized from descriptions of different sorts of experiments.

These are the objections to the claim that a string of reduction sentences could ever be an explicit definition of a dispositional predicate. Even by themselves, with no reference to previous objections, they are reason enough for denying that these predicates can be defined in terms of observational predicates.

Perhaps it will be said that I have gone too far, and that forsaking the idea of a definition provided by a string of law-statements, we can return to the original empiricist insight, and say that a single causal-law statement does provide a completely satisfactory explicit definition of a dispositional predicate. Saying that this window opens, we mean that windows of this kind always do open when sufficient force is applied. Obvious as this may seem, it is the source of the most considerable problem yet posed for Carnap's analysis of reduction sentences.

Let us suppose that Carnap's proposal for defining dispositional predicates is, as conjectured, that the definition should consist of law-statements, and let us further amend Carnap's suggestion to be that one dispositional predicate will be defined by reference to a single law-statement which has been generalized from a pair of reduction sentences. But notice: this law-statement is a counterfactual conditional, by generalizing from reduction sentences to it, we have lost the advantage of being able to distinguish true causal-law statements from counterfactuals which are false or fanciful, or are descriptions of mere accidental conjunctions. Indeed, we have come full-circle. Carnap has enabled us to distinguish among counterfactuals by stipulating that conditionals must have valid arguments if the introduction of a dispositional predicate is to be warranted; and causal-law statements have now been distinguishable, because they are the only conditionals which can satisfy the stipulations. But something has been paid out for this advantage. Causal-law statements that meet the stipulations cease to be either counterfactuals or causal-law statements; they are reduced to existential statements with valid arguments. It would have been shortsighted to have supposed that this could be a satisfactory resolution to the problem, because there was certain to be an occasion when talk about law-statements would be required, and where reference to existential statements could not be a substitute. Carnap's suggestion for providing explicit definitions for dispositional predicates has been such an occasion. We have been forced to generalize from reduction sentences, and to step up to the law-statements; but as before, we have no logical rules for separating causal-law statements, as opposed to existential ones with valid arguments, from other counterfactuals.

It must be said that Carnap's reduction sentences ultimately fail to provide the distinction we require, but that at the same time they are valuable guides to a more likely solution to our problem. Carnap's proposal is apparently one of two diametrically opposed solutions. Thus, Carnap distinguishes causal laws from other counterfactuals by making stipulations that reduction sentences must have valid arguments for certain of their variables. As we have seen, this converts true causal-law statements into existential statements, and thereby proves that the law-statements are different from other counterfactuals which cannot have all the required valid arguments. At the other extreme from this method are the purely logical attempts to distinguish among counterfactuals by manipulating the rules of material implication. These formal attempts save the generality of true causal-law statements, but it is evident that they must fail in making the needed distinction among counterfactuals, because where the issue of truth or falsity in the world counts for nothing, every counterfactual will pass any formal rule. I think that the lesson of these polar opposites is that we must incorporate the empirical evidence used by reduction sentences into a method which distinguishes among counterfactuals on logical grounds, and thereby preserves the generality of true causal statements.

IIb. 2] *Attempt to distinguish causal-law statements from other counterfactuals by showing how former can be deduced from formalized scientific systems; (a) This solution outlined, and its advantages shown.*

There is a method which does this. It proves that true causal-law statements are different from other counterfactuals by deducing them from the higher level hypotheses of an established, and formalized, scientific system; there are no comparable systems from which the other counterfactuals can be deduced. The catch to this solution is that it carries us back to a metaphysical discussion of causal necessity and potentiality. Logical empiricists sometimes propose this account, but in so doing they never admit that it commits them to a metaphysical view of the problem of dispositions. After describing the elements of the established scientific system, and the use that is made of it, I shall argue that the metaphysical implications of this solution are unavoidable.

When they are conceived logically, rather than from the vantage-point of the history of science, established scientific systems begin as logical calculi. In its essentials, a calculus has formation rules and transformation rules. Formation rules introduce the numerical variable terms, the predicate variables, the logical constants, and the operators. A well-formed formula is one in which these elements are arranged in a certain order which is arbitrarily determined, and is expressed by strings of variables, constants and operators called axioms or primitive sentences. Transformation rules limit the substitutions which can be made within an axiom and among series of axioms. They are sometimes called rules of inference, and the statement "If (AB) then (BA)" is one example of them. We apply the rules of inference when axioms are reordered into sentences called theorems of the system. Each of these theorems is said to be proved when it is the last of a series of well-formed formulae which are themselves either axioms or theorems, and when it follows from them according to the rules of inference. As it stands, this is an uninterpreted calculus. We give it an interpretation when we use it to formalize a scientific theory. In that event, each of the predicate variables is defined by reference to a class of empirical events, or is understood as one of the abstract (theoretical) terms of the theory. The logical constants are usually interpreted by reference to logical terms, such as "or," which are found in ordinary language, and the operators become universal and existential quantifiers. The highest-level hypotheses of the theory become the primitive sentences of the calculus, and its less comprehensive hypotheses are the theorems.

The formalized scientific theory is a roughly three-tiered model. The bottom tier consists of test sentences which describe particular experimental conditions and the effects which these are expected to produce. At the top are the highest-level, most general hypotheses. These explain the regularities reported by the test sentences. The middle tiers are less comprehensive hypotheses that relate the top and bottom levels.

Movement within the system can go either up or down; in either case, the movement is an inference from sentence to sentence. When we use the system deductively, transformation rules justify inferences from higher to lower sentences, and the lower level ones are said to be necessarily entailed by their premises. Inferences proceed in this way, until it comes time to instantiate from a low-level hypothesis to a test sentence. At that point, some factor in the world must be recognized. The low-level hypothesis says, For any x, if x has property A then x also has property B. The hypothesis is universally quantified, and it affirms that something is the case in all of a class of instances. This does not mean that there are any instances, for the hypothesis might describe an empty class; and therefore, we can only instantiate from the universally quantified statement when we have, or suppose that we have, an instance of Ax. This gives us the minor premise, Here is an Ax. With the hypothesis as the major premise, this entails, by *modus ponens*, the conclusion, Bx should occur. The test sentence is the conditional which has the minor premise as its antecedent and the conclusion as its consequent.

We use this sentence as a prediction of what we are likely to observe in particular circumstances. Accordingly, the test sentence turns from its logical validity, and risks empirical verification or falsification. Whichever occurs, we change directions, and consider the consequences for the higher level sentences of the system.

Let us suppose that the sentence has been verified. We now require inductive rules for measuring the significance of its verification for the higher level sentences. One thing of which we can be sure is that sentences to which we infer will not be necessary consequences of the test sentence. This cannot be the case, because the test sentence is only existentially quantified, while the hypotheses of the system are universally quantified. It is true, because the completion of a set of causal conditions was followed by the occurrence of a certain event, but this might only have been an accidental occurrence, and we cannot be certain that it will always occur when these conditions are satisfied. Even repeated successful experiments will not permit us to infer that the event will always occur. There may no longer be any question that this is the effect which occurs because these causal conditions have been satisfied, but still, the empiricists have built their Humean convictions regarding the nature of causal relations into their interpretation of the relation of existential and universally quantified statements, and under no circumstances will they admit that an effect must always occur in the future just because it has always done so in the past. Nonetheless, no one denies that verification of the test sentence confirms, in some measure, every one of the higher level hypotheses from which it was deduced, as well as all of the other hypotheses in a system in which every sentence is in more or less immediate logical relation to every other. Consequently, if the verification of one test sentence enhances the confirmation-value of the system, we have only to imagine that a multiplicity of these test sentences are verified in order to understand that a system may become almost fully confirmed.

Given this system, the means for distinguishing among counterfactuals are now readily at hand. Some counterfactuals are true, whereas others are not, because the former ones can be deduced from established scientific systems. This method is free of the disadvantage of Carnap's reduction sentences, because it does not sacrifice the generality of true causal law statements in distinguishing them from the variety of bogus counterfactuals. The method is saved from having to do that, because it does implicitly what Carnap has done explicitly. He has demanded that there should be valid arguments for sentences which justify the ascription of a dispositional predicate; but there is no reason to do this when the causal-law statements are deduced from an established system. It is unnecessary to provide valid arguments by running experiments, when a system is so highly confirmed that we can take it for granted that any sentences derived from it will be either true causal-laws or test sentences with a high likelihood of being verified.

There is but one drawback to this solution, and it may well be minor. The highest-level hypotheses of the established and formalized theory will be counterfactuals, but they will not have been deduced from any higher-level hypotheses. If the deduction of a sentence from higher-level sentences is the condition for being a causal law, it appears that these highest-level sentences are not causal laws. Perhaps the way to accommodate these exceptional cases is to point to the apparently continuous progress of science, and to suggest that we are likely to discover ever more comprehensive hypotheses from which today's and tomorrow's highest-level hypotheses will be deducible.

The most obvious, and I think the only compelling, objection to this method for distinguishing among counterfactuals is to refer to its impracticality. We do not bother to check the truth of every claim about someone's habits by deducing it from an established scientific system. Most of the time, there is no scientific theory covering circumstances of the sort being described, and very rarely do we find that an available theory has been formalized. The logical empiricists would answer this objection by admitting all that is claimed, and by adding that empiricists are only required to establish the principle: if there is a logical technique for separating valid causal-law statements from other counterfactuals, then the point is made, and a complete logical analysis of dispositional properties will have been provided. Failure to carry the method through in every case is a practical problem that has no interest for the philosopher.

IIb. 2](b) *The charge that this solution is partly an attempt to establish the metaphysical distinction between causal relationships and accidental conjunctions in space and time;* (c) *Braithwaite: general statements cannot be causal-law statements if they are confirmed exclusively by direct observation.*

This completes my survey of the so-called *logical* analysis of dispositional predicates. Empiricists are confident that their account banishes all metaphysical questions, and I now wish to prove that this is not the case. I shall argue that the established scientific system has been introduced, not only to distinguish true causal-law statements from other counter-factuals, but also, more fundamentally, in order to make sense of the categorical distinction between causal relation-ships and accidental, though constant, conjunctions. I shall also claim that the constant conjunction theory of causality, which is assumed by empiricists, affords no explanation of the fact that scientific theories become established; and that we re-quire the doctrine of causal sufficiency and necessity if we are to explain how this occurs. If this is successfully proved, it will follow that empiricist references to established scientific systems prompt us to ask metaphysical questions about poten-tiality; we recall the claim, made in the first chapter, that there would be no instances of causal sufficiency and necessity if there were no minds and objects with the potentialities for entering causal relationships.

A suggestive starting-point for our argument is the emphasis with which empiricists describe one of the identify-ing characteristics of law-statements. R. B. Braithwaite, for example, writes:

> The condition for an established hypothesis h being *lawlike* (i.e., being, if true, a natural law) will then be that the hypothesis either occurs in an established scientific deductive system as a higher-level hypothesis containing theoretical concepts or that it occurs in an established scientific deductive system as a deduction from higher-level hypotheses which are supported by empirical evidence which is not direct evidence for h itself. This condition will exclude a hypothesis for which the only evidence is evidence of instances of it, but will not exclude a hypothesis which is supported partly directly by evidence of its instances and partly indirectly by evidence of instances of same level hy-potheses.[14]

I am especially interested here in the statements that cannot be natural laws, those which are only *directly* confirmed. It is surprising to find that these are not regarded as causal-law statements. It would have seemed a reasonable view that some counterfactuals are recognized as law-statements, because there is direct evidence for them, while some others are falsified by direct evidence. This difference, with its basis in empirical fact, would be accepted from the start. Empiricists could then draw a further, and logical, distinction among the various counterfactuals by showing that some can be deduced from formalized scientific systems while others cannot. Their efforts, however, would all be subsequent to the claim, based on direct evidence alone, that certain statements are causal laws.

Braithwaite explains why he thinks this should not be said:

> A hypothesis to be regarded as a natural law must be a general proposition which can be thought to explain its instances; if the reason for believing the general proposition is solely direct knowledge of the truth of its instances, it will be felt to be a poor sort of explanation of these instances. If however, there is evidence for it which is independent of its instances, such as the indirect evidence provided by instances of a same-level hypothesis, then the general proposition will explain its instances in the sense that it will provide grounds for believing in their truth independently of any direct knowledge of such truths.[15]

The key phrase in this passage is the one where Braithwaite remarks that a general statement explains its instances when there is independent evidence for believing in the statement's truth. Remembering that indirect evidence is funded in established scientific systems by way of the verification of their test sentences, we see that Braithwaite is arguing for the view that statements must be deducible from formalized systems in order to be causal laws. Braithwaite is circumspect, but his reasons for saying this appear to be as follows. Notice first of all that Braithwaite distinguishes a proposition's truth from its standing as a causal-law statement. This is certainly justified, for the proposition that each man's breathing is preceded by the breathing of three billion others is no more a law-statement for being true and for having substantial direct evidence confirming it. But though this distinction is clear, examples like the one above pose considerable difficulties. Statements of this sort describe accidental but constant conjunctions, and there is no direct evidence which will prove that they are not causal laws. Thus, it is impossible, or almost, to arrange a test which would prove that everyone else's breathing is no causal condition of Smith's, and consequently, direct evidence is no basis for denying that the general statement covering this accidental conjunction is a causal law. And yet, everyone would agree that conjunctions of this kind are accidental, and that general statements describing them do in no way explain them. We may say that *causal laws* explain their instances, but once this is agreed, we shall have to find a way of distinguishing causal-law statements from statements describing accidental though constant conjunctions; otherwise, we shall never know whether or not an explanation is being given when someone appeals to a particular general statement. As we have seen, a statement's right to causal law status is tested by determining whether or not the statement can be deduced from an established scientific system. A proposition which is deducible will have the benefit of all the evidence which goes to confirm the system. But most of this evidence will be indirect evidence relative to the statement in question, and so Braithwaite's requirement will have been satisfied.

Though I believe that this is a fair summary of the background to Braithwaite's argument, the situation as I have just described it is not enough to account for the conclusion which Braithwaite has drawn in the passage quoted. He chooses to say that a general statement is not a causal law *unless* the statement has explanatory power, but this is to say that a statement is not a causal law unless there is indirect evidence confirming it. This is a much more extreme position than the one which we might have expected Braithwaite to adopt in these circumstances. It would have been at least as reasonable for him to have argued that some statements exclusively confirmed by direct evidence are causal laws, and that only practical, experimental difficulties stand in the way of our determining by way of direct evidence whether a particular statement is a law. This alternative approach is evidently much less subjectivistic than the view which Braithwaite favors. He argues that a statement which we are unable to confirm indirectly is not a causal law, but I am suggesting that our difficulties in finding indirect evidence for the statement are irrelevant to the fact of whether or not it is a law.

IIb. 2](d) Why Braithwaite takes this position; i. Difficulty of distinguishing causal-law statements from general statements describing accidental though constant conjunctions; ii. Difficulties in Hume's theory of causal relations; (e) Conclusions of argument: i. Empiricists rely upon formalized scientific systems when re-introducing a distinction erased by Hume; ii. Way they draw ✓ distinction presupposes reality of necessary causal connections and potentiality; c. Final evaluation of one aspect of logico-empirical analysis of dispositions.

Braithwaite fails to discuss the view which I am suggesting, but my formulation is so obviously an alternative to his own that we must suppose that Braithwaite is fully aware of this alternative, and that he has some reason for neglecting it. I want to take the liberty now of speculating about what his reason might be.

I suggest that Braithwaite is troubled by the major assumption of my analysis. I have supposed that there is a categorical distinction between the two sorts of events which are covered, respectively, by causal-law statements and statements describing accidental constant conjunctions. I would reserve the expression "causal law" for statements which describe relationships where any modification of the causal conditions would result in the modification or non-occurrence of the effect. As was argued in the first chapter, the effect is produced by, and is dependent upon its antecedent causal conditions. Accidental conjunctions are very different. There is neither production nor dependence in them, and consequently, the non-occurrence of any one of their conjuncts has no repercussions for any of the others.[16] The categorical difference between these kinds of events is the basis for a parallel distinction in the general statements which describe them. It may be impossible to determine in any particular case whether or not a statement is a law, but we had better be careful not to deny that it is, if our only reason for saying this will be that we have no indirect evidence for the statement's truth. The events described by the statement may be related by the factors of production and dependence; and if they are, this proposition will be a causal law statement however much difficulty we have in finding indirect evidence for it.

If we ask now why Braithwaite has neglected the suggestion just now made, the answer must be very clear. Braithwaite is a Humean and however much he may want to admit that wounds, for example, are *inflicted* by knives and buckshot, and that production and dependence are manifest here, he must find that these ideas are an embarrassment. Hume has said that constant conjunction is the distinguishing feature of cause and effect relations, and he has said as well that things may fall into and out of their spatial and temporal relationships without its making a difference to them or their conjuncts. Hume, rigorously applied, reduces every causal relationship to an accidental conjunction. The relation of the conjuncts may be constant, but their relationship will be no less accidental for that. There must be very few logical empiricists who follow Hume to this extreme, for most of them are as confident as the rest of us that there are genuine causal relationships in the world, and that these are different from accidental conjunctions. But the empiricists are in difficulty. They have accepted Hume's constant conjunction theory of causality despite the fact that this theory tries to eradicate the distinction they wish to acknowledge.

It is for this reason that Braithwaite ignores the suggestion that general statements may be laws when all of the evidence for them comes by way of direct observation. As Hume forces him to suppose, no general statement which is confirmed in this way is any more a causal law than any other; the events described by all of these statements are merely conjunctions in space and time.

But what sense then is Braithwaite, or any empiricist, to make of the distinction between causal-law statements and statements describing accidental constant conjunctions? How can he provide for the factors of production and dependence, and thereby justify himself when he points to an event and says that it is a causal relationship rather than an accidental conjunction? The solution is to argue as Braithwaite does when he passes over my alternative suggestion in favor of the view that statements are causal laws by virtue of our having indirect evidence of their truth. As he explains, "To consider whether or not a scientific hypothesis would, if true, be a law of nature is to consider the way in which it would enter into an established scientific system."[17] In order to interpret this, we have to suppose that a system is available, and that a statement describing the relation of certan kinds of events is deduced. This causal-law statement is a conditional, and when voiced in the subjunctive mood, it expresses the notion that a certain kind of effect would be produced if the appropriate causal conditions were fulfilled. The empiricist who affirms this statement *appears* to be in step with the rest of us. He seems to agree that conjunctions of events of the kinds described by the statement are different from accidental conjunctions. But in point of fact, this is makebelieve. The conditional statement-form and the subjunctive mood are nothing more than convenient ways of expressing the notions of production and dependence, and yet empiricists want nothing more to do with these notions once they have found the means for expressing them in their descriptions of events in the world. If asked to elaborate on the nature of the causal relationship, they will argue that accidental conjunctions and causal relationships both reduce to conjunctions in space and time, and that the difference between these relationships is only that some of them can be described — fortuitously, it must seem to them — by statements deduced from established scientific systems.

Far from rejecting metaphysics, empiricists have drawn upon scientific theories in order to reintroduce an indispensable metaphysical distinction. All of us use scientific theories to help us determine whether a particular conjunction of events is an accidental or a causal relationship, but even prior to this, and having absolutely nothing to do with assertions that they are helping scientists to clarify their concepts and assumptions, empiricists require these formalized systems in order to draw the categorical distinction between accidental conjunctions and causal relationships. Having first applied the verifiability principle to eliminate causal sufficiency and necessity from the world, empiricists use scientific theories as a means for thinking of the world as if production and existential dependence were factors in it.

David Hume himself could not have been more orthodox. He argued that the production and dependence which we ascribe to cause and effect relations are no more than the mind's determination to think the idea of an effect when we have the impression or idea of its cause, and he insisted that it is only these acquired habits of association which prompt us to think of the world as if order were deeply rooted in it. Contemporary empiricists agree that causal sufficiency and necessity have no reality in the world, but, and here they deviate slightly from Hume, they argue that we can think of the world as if these formal elements have a place in it because there are formalized scientific systems. Pap makes this very clear:

> Yet, it remains to be seen whether one could not do justice to the feeling that there is some sort of "necessary connection" between cause and effect without introducing an unanalyzed notion of "causal entailment." It may be that to feel there is a necessity for the effect to follow the cause is merely to suspect that the observed regular sequence can be explained in the sense

of being deducible from certain empirical premises. Thus, we feel that the heating of a block of ice must eventually be followed by melting of the ice. We express this feeling by saying "if the ice were heated, it would melt, no matter whether it ever will be heated and no matter whether such a sequence is ever observed by anybody." Now, if a physicist were asked why he thinks the melting is necessitated by the heating, he would undoubtedly make the following sort of reply: "that a heated block of ice must, other factors being equal, melt, follows from the fact that in heating a solid substance one increases the kinetic energy of its molecules and thereby enables the molecules to overcome the cohesive forces which hold them together and give the substance the appearance of being solid." Wherein lies the necessity here? In nothing else but the logical consequence of the causal law from a physical theory.[18]

This is a faithful representation, I believe, of the approach that all logical empiricists would have us adopt in these matters, and indeed it shows that empiricists have taken the step that Hume was always loathe to take. He was prepared to admit that causal necessity is operative in the workings of the mind. Pap, however, is willing to dismiss the determinations of the mind as mere feelings, and to draw causal necessity from the mind just as Hume has already drawn it from the world. Empiricists reassure us that nothing is lost on either count, because we can read necessity back into the world, and presumably back into the order of our conceptions, by consulting the scientific systems which are the empiricists' formal replicas of experience. The liability which empiricists never mention is that necessity has all been packed into the model; with none remaining for thought or nature, thought should be too incoherent to make use of these models, and chaos in the world should belie the order which the models ascribe to nature.

Empiricists certainly have a very different notion of

their procedure from the one which I have expressed. They never say that formal systems are used as a crutch for making a metaphysical distinction; how could that be true when every metaphysical problem is a confusion? Stern application of the verifiability principle is said to have disposed of these classic philosophic misconceptions, and only logical considerations are thought to remain. It is obvious to empiricists that problems of this sort will have to be analyzed by reference to formal systems.

I hope to have established that this latter is a short-sighted view of the empiricist program, and as I now want to argue, it is much too optimistic an evaluation of empiricist achievements. The attempt to distinguish causal-law statements from other counterfactuals is our case in point. There has been no pretense of drawing the required distinction by stipulating that the causal law statements must be deducible from just any logical system. To the contrary, the system must be one which accurately explains and predicts phenomena in the world; it must be an established system. Notice however, that we only grant that a theory is established when its predictions are invariably confirmed, and we mean by this that the particular causal conditions described in the various predictions derived from a theory must always produce an anticipated effect. If, however, it is true, as the empiricisis say, that there is no production and dependence in nature, there will be no reason why anticipated effects should occur when causal conditions are satisfied. As Hume has said, anything could happen. It is hardly likely that predicted effects would occur, or consequently, that predictions would be verified. In order to explain why some predictions are verified, we have to reject the theory of constant conjunction, accepting instead the doctrine of necessary connection. There appears to be no other theory that accounts for the recurrent patterns of change which we find in experience. Nor is there any other that explains how scientific systems come to be established.[19]

The fact of real potentiality will be the unavoidable next inference. We must refer to it in order to explain why certain things rather than others constitute the sets of causal conditions which produce effects, and thereby verify predictions. With the recognition that there is potentiality in the world, we can say that the empiricists have not provided an adequate substitute for the realist analysis of dispositional properties. To say that something is disposed to effect or suffer some change will mean, as before, that it has the potentiality for doing that.

When we survey this reductionist theory of dispositional properties, one feature in particular would seem to account for the persuasiveness which the analysis has for many people. This is the fact that the causal-law statement analysis has been very successful in representing the characteristic openness of powers. It has identified this factor with the procedure of deriving existential conditional statements by way of *modus ponens*; these conditionals can be derived whenever there is a valid argument for the antecedent of the causal-law statement. So perfect an expression of a significant feature of dispositions has been seized upon by the empiricists as very strong evidence in favor of their analysis.

We are in a position now to see that the empiricists have capitalized on what is really the most fortuitous of accidents. They have sought to analyze a characteristic feature of potentialities, and a simple logical technique has provided exactly what is required. It is evident, however, that there is an important disparity between this device and the powers of things in the world. The logical relation between a causal-law statement and the conditionals derived from it is, of course, a purely formal relation, and consequently, we can take advantage of this relation by imagining any number of spurious causal laws, supposing that there are valid arguments for their antecedents and deducing that there must be a valid argument for the consequent as well. We can repeat this imaginary derivation as often as we please, and formally, at least, there will be nothing to distinguish the dispositions of the things we imagine from the powers of minds and objects in the world; both will have the openness that we attribute to dispositional properties.

The empiricist response must be that we can distinguish the bogus from the valid ascriptions of dispositional properties by showing that only certain of the causal-law statements can be deduced from established scientific systems. This, however, is to admit defeat. In the first place, it admits that one requires some method beyond application of the rule of *modus ponens* to establish that openness has been rightly attributed to a genuine disposition, and, second, it opens the empiricist to the charge that he presupposes all of the metaphysical assumptions which he would so much like to eliminate, for, as I have argued, no theory would ever become established if production, dependence, and potentiality were not factors in the world.

In order to begin this lengthy discussion in good faith, we had to concede that our intuitive convictions about powers might be mistaken. This makes it particularly satisfying to have proved that there is no philosophic justification for rejecting those intuitions, and none for saying, in opposition to Austin, that things can act only when they are actually performing.

3

THE EXISTENCE
OF NONINTROSPECTABLE MENTAL STATES

IIIa. Introduction: We hope to prove existence of factors constituting actuality of minds similar to mass and shape which constitute actuality of bodies; B. *Account of Wittgenstein's later theory;* 1] *Wittgenstein's conception of mind;* (a) *Behaviorism;* (b) *Criticisms of nonintrospectable mental states;* (c) *Proof that Wittgenstein is a behaviorist.*

Having secured the ideas of causal sufficiency and necessity and of power against the criticisms of Hume and the logical empiricists, I want to return to the development of the realist theory. One question in particular demands our attention: I have suggested in Chapter 1, when talking about the nonintrospectable states and capacities of minds, that things have powers, because of the properties which constitute their actuality. This is an obvious claim to make about the powers of physical objects at least; we recognize, for example, that a well-honed knife has the power to cut because of the sharpness of its blade. On the other hand, it is not so obvious that there is a comparable relation between the nonintrospectable states and powers of minds. Indeed, many persons deny that minds have these states at all. It is my own belief that nonintrospectable mental states do exist, and that they function relative to mental powers in the same way as shape, for instance, functions in relation to the powers of physical objects. Moreover, in Chapter 4, I shall try to determine the precise character of the relation which holds between actuality and potentiality in minds and objects. For the present, however, I want merely to prove that minds do have nonintrospectable states. It will be much easier to account in Chapter 4 for mind's possession of its powers if this is established now.

My procedure here will be to consider one example of a theory of mind which supposes that nonintrospectable mental states do not exist. I shall argue that the theory in question is incapable of providing a complete explanation of mental activity just because it makes this assumption. The class of theories which I have in mind are called "behaviorist," holding as they do that all descriptive terms pertinent to talk about minds can be exhaustively defined from the standpoint of an observer who describes the bodily motions and acts of speech which other persons have learned as appropriate responses to particular circumstances. It seems to me that Ludwig Wittgenstein adopted a behaviorist view of mind in his later writings, and I shall argue for the existence of nonintrospectable mental states by way of a criticism of Wittgenstein's conception of mind. There will be two parts to the discussion. The first part will be a brief review of the principal elements of Wittgenstein's behaviorism, and the second will attempt to resurrect the notion of mental states in the face of Wittgenstein's objections to what he disparages as "hidden" mental mechanisms. In this second part, I shall emphasize the epistemological assumptions which prompt Wittgenstein to deny that mental states exist.

Wittgenstein, in his later work, devotes much of his attention to occasions on which various mental activities are learned, because the alternative, a description of the behavior of the accomplished technician, would have to penetrate extraneous detail in order to expose essential features of mental activity which are already apparent in the learning situation. Wittgenstein justifies his procedure in this way:

It disperses the fog to study the phenomena of language in primitive kinds of application in which one can command a clear view of the aim and functioning of the words. A child uses such primitive forms of language when it learns to talk. Here the teaching of language is not explanation, but training.[1]

There is another passage in which Wittgenstein describes the general features of the learning situation, and, given the point of the sentences just quoted, thereby draws our attention to what he regards as the significant factors of mental activity. He writes:

In the course of this teaching, I shall show him (the learner) the same colours, the same lengths, the same shapes, I shall make him find them and produce them and so on. I shall, for instance, get him to continue an ornamental pattern uniformly when told to do so. — And also to continue progressions. And so, for example, when given: . .. ... to go on: .... I do it, he does it after me; and I influence him by expressions of agreement, rejection, expectation, encouragement. I let him go his way, or hold him back; and so on.[2]

And Wittgenstein adds,

But if a person has not yet got the concepts, I shall teach him to use the words by means of examples and by practice. — And when I do this I do not communicate less to him that I know myself.[3]

These remarks emphasize three factors in the learning situation: the particular circumstances to which the student is trained to react; the conduct with which he is to respond to them; and the pleasure or pain which encourages an appropriate response and discourages unsatisfactory ones. Wittgenstein also suggests or implies that there are several practical teaching devices, such as repetition of the lessons, regularity in the circumstances to which the student is to respond, and properly timed and sufficiently intense rewards and punishments. These are the factors which constitute the learning situation, and, significantly, no empiricist could be offended by them. The student is encouraged to perform overt acts of behavior in response to particular circumstances which are features of a publicly observable environment, and his responses are encouraged or discouraged by an instructor who gives overt evidence of his requirements. The pleasure or pain experienced by a student will be described as a satisfied glow, a grimace, or as an utterance or bodily movement.

Reinforcement and the practical teaching-devices are more prominent in training than they are when a skill has been acquired, but they add no great complexity to the learning situation, and we can readily distinguish them from the act of responding to particular circumstances, the essence of skilled activity so far as behaviorists are concerned. Wittgenstein is one of the philosophers who agrees that this is all that counts in mental activity, and he concentrates upon the learning situation, because, as he thinks, there is no opportunity here for describing mind in terms of factors that are irrelevant to it.

Two of his comments show that Wittgenstein regards unobservable mental mechanisms as prime examples of the factors with no legitimate place in a description of mental activity:

> Imagine that human beings or animals were used as reading machines: assume that in order to become reading machines they need a particular training . . . (In this case) by calling certain creatures "reading machines" we meant only that they react in a particular way to seeing printed signs. No connection between seeing and reacting, no internal mechanism enters into this case. . . . The change which took place was one which we might call a change in the general behavior of the pupil.[4]

And in a similar vein,

> But in the case of the living reading-machines "reading" meant reacting to written signs in such-and-such ways.

This concept was therefore quite independent of that of a mental or other mechanism.[5]

The "mental mechanisms" referred to in these passages could as easily be conscious mental states as the nonintrospectable ones which occupy us here. It makes no difference to Wittgenstein whether we interpret the phrase in one way or the other; in either event, he supposes that mental mechanisms have no legitimate part in a description of reading. Reading, like every other mental activity, is merely the behavior which has been learned as the appropriate response to particular circumstances.

This is not all that Wittgenstein has to say about mental activity; yet this is the crux of his argument. Other points which he makes in talking of activities like reading are normally intended to defend his behaviorist position against arguments which would supplement the behaviorist view with references to either conscious or nonintrospectable mental states. In every case, Wittgenstein rejects these arguments. One passage summarizes his view of all attempts to show that mental activity is more than overt behavior. He writes:

> Now we should of course like to say: What goes on in that practiced reader and in the beginner when they utter the word can't be the same. And if there is no difference in what they happen to be conscious of there must be one in the unconscious workings of their minds, or, again, in the brain. — So we should like to say: There are at all events two different mechanisms at work here. And what goes on in them must distinguish reading from not reading. — But *these mechanisms are only hypotheses, models designed to explain, to sum up, what you observe.*[6] (Italics supplied.)

This passage mentions three theories of mental activity which offer something in addition to a description of overt behavior; all of them explain the occurrence of overt behavior by referring to various kinds of mental states. There are introspectionist explanations which talk about conscious states;

explanations which regard mind as essentially a nonintrospectable structure after the manner of Leibniz, Kant and the faculty psychologists; and physiological explanations. So far as Wittgenstein is concerned, each of these is no more than a fanciful gloss upon a description of overt behavior. When the alternatives show pretensions of telling us things which no behaviorist could ever hope to tell, Wittgenstein rejects them.[7]

Nothing then remains but his simple, behaviorist account of mental activity:

> Try not to think of understanding as a "mental process" at all. — For *that* is the expression which confuses you. But ask yourself; in what sort of case, in what kind of circumstances, do we say, "Now I know how to go on," when, that is, the formula has occurred to me? In the sense in which there are processes (including mental processes) which are characteristic of understanding, understanding is not a mental process. (A pain's growing more and less: the hearing of a tune or a sentence: these are mental processes.)

And from earlier in this paragraph:

> If there has to be anything "behind the utterance of the formula" it is *particular circumstances* which justify me in saying I can go on — when the formula occurs to me.[8]

Wittgenstein, it seems to me, could only be classified as a stimulus-and-response behaviorist.

There are many Wittgensteinians who vigorously dispute this claim. They say that Wittgenstein's theory of language requires him to talk in ways that may seem behavioristic, but that, in fact, Wittgenstein is by no means a behaviorist. A brief review of Wittgenstein's theory of language will help us to evaluate their interpretation.

Wittgenstein opposes what he regards as the traditional view that linguistic expressions have meanings by virtue of naming things that exist either in consciousness or the public world. He rejects this theory because conscious states such as affections, acts of understanding and volitions cannot be displayed, and therefore cannot be publicly correlated with the expressions which are supposed to be their names. To Wittgenstein's mind, this entails that expressions like "pain" should have as many meanings as there are individuals who understand the term as referring to their own unique sensations. But if this were true, he argues, "pain," and every term whose object was a conscious state, would have no common meaning, and it would be impossible to communicate about one's pains and such to other people. Solipsism would be the result if this theory of language were true. Obviously, however, we are able to tell others about our pains, desires and things we know, and, consequently, the theory of language which is said to entail the impossibility of communication must be in error.[9]

The theory which Wittgenstein would substitute for his version of the traditional one is that linguistic expressions are meaningful, because there are rules, learned by all of us, for correctly using the expressions. We learn to use "pain," for example, not by correlating it with a sensation, but rather by practicing the use of the expression in particular circumstances. Wittgenstein goes so far as to argue that proper names are meaningful only because they have a use. Thus, he says that ". . . naming is something like attaching a label to a thing. One can say that this is preparatory to the use of a word."[10] And:

> Let us now imagine a use for the entry of the sign "E" in my diary. . . . And what is our reason for calling "E" the name of a sensation here? Perhaps the kind of way this sign is employed in this language-game. — And why a "particular sensation," that is, the same one every time? Well, aren't we supposing that we write "E" every time?[11]

Names are the expressions whose meanings are least likely to be their uses, and by arguing that names have no meaning apart from their use, Wittgenstein intends to sweep away any remnant of the traditional theory. No exception is made; not even for the demonstrative "this," that term which has some-times been regarded as the purest example of a name.[12] In every case, the meaning of a term will be the rules for its use.

Having this conception of language, Wittgenstein in-sists that mental states, and particularly the conscious ones, have no significance for the meanings of linguistic expres-sions. As he puts it:

> Now someone tells me that *he* knows what pain is only from his own case! — Suppose everyone had a box with something in it: we call it a "beetle." No one can look into anyone else's box, and everyone says he knows what a beetle is only by looking at *his* beetle. — Here it would be quite possible for everyone to have something dif-ferent in his box. One might even imagine such a thing constantly changing. — But suppose the word "beetle" had a use in these people's language? — If so it would not be used as the name of a thing. The thing in the box has no place in the language-game at all; not even as a *something*: for the box might even be empty. — No, one can "divide through" by the thing in the box; it cancels out, whatever it is. That is to say: *If we con-strue the grammar of the expression of sensation on the model of "object and name" the object drops out of consideration as irrelevant.* (Italics supplied.)[13]

Wittgenstein's point is that the idiosyncrasies of our indi-vidual mental states are irrelevant when all of us have ac-cepted a particular rule for using an expression in ordinary speech.

Philosophers who deny that Wittgenstein is a behav-iorist argue that he is only regarded as one by people who mistakenly suppose that remarks like the one about the "beetle" are intended as characterizations of all experience, and not just of language. Norman Malcolm tries to expose this "misconception" by quoting various passages in which Wittgenstein talks of activities such as describing and giving names to sensations, and Malcolm concludes that "It is a howler to accuse Wittgenstein of 'hostility to the idea of what is not observed.' "[14]

Unfortunately, none of the passages to which he refers can be accepted as evidence for Malcolm's interpretation of Wittgenstein. Malcolm assumes that Wittgenstein would have us understand his use of expressions like "describing," "naming," "reporting," and "recognizing" as if these expressions were intended as references to conscious mental states. But evidently it is too late to impute this intention to Wittgenstein when the man has unequivocally told us that talk about naming, describing, reporting and recognizing has nothing to do with conscious states. Wittgenstein has said categorically that these objects are "irrelevant" to the use of these expressions, and that we can properly use the expressions even if there are no conscious states occurring in people's heads. Under the circumstances, no passage in which Wittgenstein talks about sensations, dreams, or whatever can be regarded as a reference to conscious mental states, hence, no passage can be quoted as evidence that Wittgenstein is not hostile to experiences which cannot be observed.

Indeed, one of Wittgenstein's own remarks testifies that he does not regard conscious states as being any part of human experience. He asks one rhetorical question, and answers it with a second:

> "So if a man has not learned a language, is he unable to have certain memories?" Of course — he cannot have verbal memories, verbal wishes or fears, and so on. And memories, etc., in language, are not mere threadbare representations of the *real* experiences; for is what is linguistic not an experience?[15]

But if language is experience, and linguistic expressions are merely the utterances which are learned as responses to particular circumstances, there is no avoiding the claim that Wittgenstein is a straightforward example of a stimulus-response behaviorist.

The next question that I want to raise is this: why does

Wittgenstein take up a behaviorist position and say that mental states, and in particular nonintrospectable ones, do not exist? The attempt to answer this question and prove that Wittgenstein is mistaken will occupy the remainder of this chapter.

IIIb. 2] *Empiricist assumptions underlying Wittgenstein's account of mind;* (a) *Behaviorism as an observer-centered theory of mental activity;* (b) *Wittgenstein's responses to the problem of verification;* 3] *Unacceptable consequences of Wittgenstein's behaviorism.*

There are several paragraphs which lead us directly to the answer to our question, and these I want to quote or summarize before commenting upon them. Among the most revealing passages are those where Wittgenstein describes a dialogue between an instructor who is teaching someone how to read, and an observer who occasionally guesses whether the student has now learned the technique. The problem for the instructor and the observer is to determine when it is proper to say that the student has finally learned how to read; and Wittgenstein writes:

> Which was the first word, or the first letter which he read? It is clear that this question here makes no sense unless I give an "artificial" explanation such as: "The first word which he reads=the first word of the first hundred consecutive words he reads correctly."[16]

And similarly,

> "Perhaps he was already reading when he said that word." For there is no doubt about what he did — The change when the pupil began to read was a change in his behavior; it makes no sense here to speak of "a first word in his new state."[17]

Our problem is to determine, by way of an analysis of these paragraphs, why it should be meaningless to say that a learner has read when he has only made a single correct utterance, or the first of a series of correct utterances. It certainly is not obvious that this is the case: parents frequently say this about young childen, and though they are quite often mistaken, it seems to be the case that their assertions are at least meaningful. Why, then, does Wittgenstein argue to the contrary?

The beginnings of an answer are to be found in the perspective from which these paragraphs describe the activities of the learner. All of the discussion centers upon the student and his performance, but at the same time this is not a clinical report of a matter of fact. The details of the situation filter through to us by way of the conversation of the two people who have taken up positions relative to the student, and are observing and reporting on him. This characteristic of the paragraph is not merely accidental to it. Wittgenstein would prefer that we discuss mental activities, like reading, from the vantage point of the observer; even more, he supposes that there is *no* other perspective. The reason for this is that behaviorism is an observer-centered view of mental activity. It is the theory that mental activities are exclusively or best described from the vantage point of a man taking notes on the overt behavior of his fellows.

Once we adopt Wittgenstein's viewpoint, the structure of his argument becomes somewhat clearer. The student is the nominal object of interest, and he is always the point of reference for the discussion. But at the same time, emphasis is drawn from him to the observers. Wittgenstein is fundamentally concerned to tell us what the observers can and cannot say about the learner, and, most of all, to insist that it is "senseless" for them to say that the student has read the first word which he correctly utters.

It is "senseless," I think, because Wittgenstein is tacitly referring to that earlier training-period when the observers learned how to respond to people or machines who are learning to read. At that time, the observers learned to say "He is reading" as a response to reading machines which made a certain number of correct utterances. And now, when he is presumed to have mastered that technique, it is "senseless" for the observer to use this sentence when the pupil has made only a single correct utterance, because the observer has deviated from the rule that he was trained to follow. The rule prescribes that this sentence is only to be uttered when a student makes a series of correct noises when looking at a printed page; and responding with the sentence on other occasions is "senseless," because it is inappropriate. Another man who has been trained to follow this rule is likely to hear the observer's remark, and look for the particular circumstances that should have prompted it. But he would not find them, even supposing that he had a recording of the student's performance; and the remark would not mean anything to him, because he could not tie it to the circumstances that are the condition for justifiably making it. In essence, the observer's remark is meaningless, because it is an idle noise when uttered out of its appropriate context.

I understand that a Wittgensteinian might caution against making too much of the reputed senselessness of utterances which are made in uncommon circumstances; particularly since Wittgenstein stipulates that he is describing reading machines in these passages. If a normally meaningful statement is meaningless on occasions when we are looking at a robot that is not much of a loss. Surely however, this is too charitable an interpretation. It is strange that a statement can lose its meaning just because of a peculiarity in the circumstances in which it is uttered, and moreover, there is little reason to suppose that Wittgenstein's charge of meaninglessness would be withdrawn if the learner were a child rather than a reading machine. This is true for three reasons. The first, and most obvious is that Wittgenstein himself has suggested that we should consider "human beings or creatures of some other kind"[18] as reading-machines. Second, and rather more important, we may consider the training of the observer who makes the reputedly meaningless utterance. The observer has learned to say "He is reading" in circumstances where someone or something makes appropriate noises when a page having marks on it is placed in front of him. The physical appearance of the person or thing making these noises might be a factor in the circumstances which prompt the observer to make his remark, but even if this were so, the observer could be easily fooled by dressing up the robot. Under the circumstances, it would make no difference to the observer whether the reader were a child or a machine. For the third point, we must recall that Wittgenstein's behaviorist account of mental activity stresses the notion of stimulus and response to the exclusion of all other considerations. On this view, there is no difference in principle between the activities of people and those of sophisticated machines which are constructed to respond as humans do. For all three of these reasons, Wittgenstein's claim about the observer's utterance must be taken seriously.

Wittgenstein himself cures us of any lingering doubts that we may have on this issue, when he generalizes the conclusion of the passages in which the reading machine is discussed. We are now told that there must be substantial evidence before we can say of any activity that it has been performed successfully. Wittgenstein writes:

> Is what we call "obeying a rule" something that it would be possible for only one man to do, and to do only once in his life? — This is of course a note on the grammar of the expression "to obey a rule." It is not possible that there should have been only one occasion on which someone obeyed a rule. It is not possible that there should have been only one occasion on which a report was made, an order given or understood; and so on. — To obey a rule, to make a report, to give an order, to play a game of chess, are *customs* (uses, institutions). To understand a sentence means to understand a language. To understand a language means to be master of a technique.[19]

The standpoint adopted in the passages describing the reading machines is apparently the one from which this paragraph is also written. On the one hand, Wittgenstein makes a claim about the moves, orders, and reports that people make. On the other, he emphasizes the grammar of the expression which observers use in talking about activities like these.

At the level of observed fact, Wittgenstein argues that it is not possible that there could have been only one occasion on which some rule was obeyed. A rule would not be a rule, he believes, if it were obeyed just once; a prescription or direction only becomes a rule when it is followed a number of times. Similarly, acting in a certain way is not regarded as an instance of rule-following if the action is performed only once. Rule-following is a custom, and one must perform several times before a certain kind of action is acknowledged to be an example of rule-following. By definition then, a single, unrepeated performance will not count as obeying a rule, and the direction which determined the form of the action will not count as a rule.

Shifting to the level of the observer, I interpret Wittgenstein to mean that the observer has mastered the technique for using the phrase "to obey a rule," in circumstances where the subjects of observation made numerous moves, utterances, orders or reports. This, it seems to me, is the implication of the remark that Wittgenstein is only commenting upon the grammar of the phrase "to obey a rule"; the grammar of an expression is the rule of its use, and the rule prescribes that the expression should only be used in circumstances resembling those in which the rule was learned. Thus if it is the grammar of the expression "to obey a rule" that rules cannot be obeyed just once, this means that the rule for using this expression was learned in circumstances where people were observed as they made numerous utterances, moves and reports.

On this interpretation, the phrase "to obey a rule" would be used inappropriately if it were uttered in circumstances where a man who had invented a game, made the first move, and then destroyed the rules, never to play again. Presumably, the observer's remark that a rule had been obeyed would be equally out of place if it were made at the time of the first of a long series of moves in the new game.

Remembering that "He is reading" was said to be meaningless under these circumstances, we can reasonably suppose that "He obeyed a rule" would also be. I think this is a fair inference to draw, because, in addition to his remark in connection with the reading machines, Wittgenstein has said that "it is not possible" for us to say that a rule has been obeyed when there has been only a single example of the correct behavior.

Our problem at this juncture is to explain why it is that Wittgenstein emphasizes the meaninglessness of utterances which are made on certain occasions. Wittgenstein's own explanation is that he is commenting upon the grammar of the expression "to obey a rule," but I suggest that more is at stake. The limitations imposed upon the use of this expression, and less general ones like "He is reading," are a way of acknowledging the behaviorist's inability to verify certain claims about mental activity. This awkward situation develops, because Wittgenstein describes mental activity as nothing more than the making of appropriate responses to particular circumstances. Numerous correct utterances or moves are sufficient to convince him that a student has mastered a rule, but Wittgenstein must be chary about committing himself on the first one or few correct responses, because his behaviorism makes it impossible for him to tell whether a student's first correct responses are proof that he has learned a rule, or are mere lucky guesses. Wittgenstein approaches the issue very cautiously as he remarks that, ". . . we have not given a meaning to the expression 'the first word in the new era.' "[20]

The behaviorist has several choices open to him on these occasions. He may decide to give more credence to introspectionist evidence, and he may then ask the student whether he feels confident that his performance is evidence that he has mastered the rule; or he may put his faith in physiological research in the hope that scientists will some day find that there is a modification in the brains of students who have mastered a technique. And possibly, the behaviorist may recognize the legitimacy of all the various sources of information about the student, but discover that he is still forced to admit that he does not have enough evidence to tell whether or not the student has learned the rule.

As it happens, Wittgenstein rejects all of these possibilities. He prefers to argue in such a way that the problem of verification disappears. There are two factors to be covered if this is to be done convincingly. 1] The first is to argue that a single performance does not constitute an act of reading, chess-playing, or whatever. This is the point made when Wittgenstein supposes that rule-following is an institution or custom. As I suggested above, it becomes a matter of definition that a single utterance cannot be an instance of obeying a rule. 2] The second line of argument is to say that sentences reporting that a student has caught on to a rule are only learned as responses to lengthy performances. Making this stipulation, Wittgenstein can suppose that the sentence is only meaningfully used in circumstances where there is sufficient evidence to confirm the assertion. After these points have been made, there can be no problem of verification. We do not have to determine whether the proposition "He is reading" has been truly affirmed of a student's behavior, if first utterances cannot, by definition, be instances of reading. Moreover, there is no problem of verifying a proposition which turns out to be meaningless when used in circumstances like these.

It seems evident to me that this is totally unsatisfactory. Contrary to the frequent claim that Wittgenstein has no interest in reforming ordinary language,[21] we find him arguing that ordinary language assertions are meaningless when their truth cannot be determined by the observer of overt behavior. This verificationist motive is in fact the explanation for so many of Wittgenstein's efforts to convince us that we ought not to interpret our assertions in the ways that we do normally interpret them. The statement "I am in pain," meaning that I have a throbbing headache over the left eye, is an example. Wittgenstein would eliminate all such interpretations of these utterances, because no observer can verify them. And this is not just an inference. Wittgenstein makes it very clear why he dislikes these interpretations:

> The essential thing about private experience is really not that each person possesses his own exemplar, but that nobody knows whether other people also have *this* or something else. The assumption would thus be possible — though unverifiable — that one section of mankind had one sensation of red and another section another.[22]

When the difficulties of verifying statements about mental activities become very great, it is simpler for the behaviorist to make the problem evaporate by supposing that assertions are meaningless when they are uttered on occasions where there is little or no evidence for their truth. This, as I have tried to prove, is just the supposition which Wittgenstein makes.

I suggest that the error of this view is a failure to distinguish what the subject of observation (the learner in this case) is doing from what the observer is doing. Wittgenstein clearly knows the difference between a learner's reading and an observer's looking, but the claim is that his preoccupation with verifiability has led Wittgenstein mistakenly to identify the observer's effort as the logically prior of the two activities. For example, the student tries to read, and the observer aims to discover whether or not he has succeeded. This way of putting it makes the observer's activity dependent upon the student's. The student performs, and the observer squints and wonders if this is evidence that a technique has been mastered. Wittgenstein, however, has reversed the order of dependence.

He appears to reason as follows: If there is little or no evidence that a student has read, then there is no reason for believing that an assertion such as "He is reading" is true. From this, Wittgenstein concludes that talk about the student's reading lapses into senselessness. But further, when we cannot meaningfully say that a man is reading, the very issue dissolves before us, and a matter of objective fact is annihilated just because the observer has been unable to determine what has occurred. All the power of Wittgenstein's argument has gone to support the requirements of the observer, and as a result, he makes the unacceptable claim that normally meaningful utterances become meaningless when the observer cannot determine whether they are true.

IIIc. A substitute for Wittgenstein's theory; 1] A non-behavioral account of mental activity; Kant's three-fold synthesis: apprehension, reproduction and recognition.

There is an alternative to Wittgenstein's observer-centered account of mental activity, and I suggest that it is more credible than his view. Suppose that a bright but petulant child is taught to read, and that after several lessons, she refuses to go on. We, the observers, are left to puzzle over the few correct utterances which she did make during the lessons, but which she will not be cajoled into making again. I do not think we would say, with Wittgenstein, that it is not meaningful, and hence that it cannot be true to say that she did read. We are more likely to say that we do not have sufficient evidence to decide the issue. We say this, because we recognize that there are three distinguishable, and, indeed, separable, considerations here. There is the objective fact of the child's success or failure; there is the asserting of a proposition whose predicate characterizes utterances which are correct responses to marks on a page; and there is the observer eager to know if the predicate truly characterizes the actions of this child. It is possible that the proposition is true, and if so, it will remain true whether or not the observer satisfies himself that it is.

If we accept these distinctions we also necessarily deny that it is meaningless to talk about mental activity in circumstances where we cannot be sure that it has taken place. We repudiate verifiability as our controlling principle because it limits talk about mental activities to descriptions of numerous responses to particular circumstances.

This is the first step in the direction of a new theory of

mental activity, but it cannot be the last; we say that verifiability is not to be our governing principle, but we have continued to assume, as is unnecessary I think, that activities like reading should be described from the vantage-point of the observer. Thus reading, in the last example, can be described merely as reponse to marks on a page by means of an appropriate utterance. We have still to prove that there can be descriptions of mental activity which make no provision for the observer, and another example shows that this is the case.

We imagine a child who is shy but clever, and who learns to read without ever practicing aloud; close attention to the behavior of others and imaginative rehearsal are quite sufficient to enable him to read. This is conceivable and as a matter of fact it occurs frequently. We are often surprised at how well a child performs when he first demonstrates that he can read. Suppose that we make it our problem to define "reading" in terms of this example.

The behaviorist will suggest that the primary definition of "reading" is "the making of appropriate noises in response to confrontation with a printed page," and (in order to cover people who normally read silently) he will add the proviso that someone who is reading to himself would make the appropriate noises "on demand." Clearly, however, this behaviorist definition has no obvious relevance to the reading of the child in our example, or to adults who have been reading close-lipped for years. The closest that the definition comes to having any bearing upon our example is to imply that there is no justification for saying that the child did read quietly to himself, unless the child will read aloud if asked to do so. The trouble with this requirement is that it is merely another expression of the verifiability principle. As we have already distinguished the fact of someone's reading from the fact of our trying to discover whether he has read, this consideration has no legitimate part in a definition of "reading"; and, consequently, as there is nothing to recommend in this behaviorist definition, we can reject it out of hand.

What we require is a definition which makes no concession to behaviorist requirements. This is to say that there need be no place in our definition for the idea that reading is noisemaking or some other sort of overt behavior. A reference to noisemaking is unnecessary, because, as our example purports to show, reading is not noisemaking or the prospect of noisemaking. Reading aloud is encouraged for instructional purposes; teachers want to know if their students are catching on. When they subsequently discourage the students from reading aloud, teachers are not asking them to forget how to read.

I suggest that a suitable definition, one making no reference to overt behavior, is that reading is the understanding of words printed on things like pages and billboards. This is surely a commonplace definition, and yet, the implications of the notion of understanding are by no means as simple as behaviorists would have us believe. Responding properly to particular circumstances is sometimes a symptom of understanding, and very often the symptom is all that concerns us, but still, this is not all or even the heart of intellectual activity. For a detailed account of the fundamentals of this activity, it seems to me that Immanuel Kant is the man to whom we must turn.

He describes the categorical features of mental activity in the Transcendental Deduction of the First Edition of the *Critique of Pure Reason*. This is the section where he writes of the threefold synthesis of apprehension, reproduction and recognition. Kant's ultimate purpose in this section is to prove that experience must be unified, or, to borrow from one of Whitehead's remarks, to prove that consciousness is like the idea of a sequence, and is not only a sequence of ideas. The threefold synthesis is said to be the mode of activity of the *transcendental unity of apperception*, and as an expression of this prior unity, it is thought to be a condition for the unity of our conscious experience. Many philosophers have denied the legitimacy of the idea of transcendental apperception, but none, I think, has been able to show that the threefold synthesis is any less essential to the coherence and intelligibility of experience than Kant makes it out to be.

The syntheses themselves amount to this: apprehension

is the seeing of particular, but successive, moments of experience as bound up in the unity of time. With reading as our example, this means that the words on a page can be read in a meaningful sequence, because our apprehension of the *duration* of time makes it possible for us to discern the relations among words written in sentences. In order to see this more clearly, let us consider the alternative view. Suppose that our experience of time were atomistic, and that we apprehended as many times as there are discrete and separable events succeeding one another in experience. If this were the case, the problem would be to show how these temporal atoms come to be linked up in relations of precedence and succession, and subsequently, in relations of meaning. It would be most important that there be such an explanation, because, as matters would stand, the reading of every word would be a completely isolated act having no relation to the reading of other words in a sentence. There would be no such thing as a two-word phrase, and words having many syllables would break up into isolated and unrelated parts. As it happens, there appears to be no way of accounting for the intelligibility of self-conscious mental life on the assumption that our experience of time is atomistic. To avoid the untenable conclusion that reflective experience is a heap of unrelated impressions and ideas, we must return to our original claim and say with Kant that there is a synthesis enabling the mind to apprehend the duration spanning the plurality of events successively experienced by the mind.

Reproduction, or memory, is the second synthesis, and it accounts for the fact that every step in an intellectual activity has a definite relevance to it, as would not be the case if we were unaware of the steps that had gone before. For want of this synthesis, all of us would at every moment be as if we had forgotten what we were about to say in the very act of saying it. Only one reservation has to be made. "Reproduction" implying the figurative imagining of things once experienced suggests more than Kant intends. Imagining of a previous experience is sometimes necessary, but cases like this are exceptional. It is enough for the understanding if the mind acts out of cognizance of what has gone before, and this is normally guaranteed by the mechanical association of our ideas. To imagine the immediately previous event would usually be a wasted effort, and so we rarely do it.

Reproduction has obvious significance for reading; it cannot be said that we know what we are reading, unless every word and every sentence is understood to come when it does, because of what has gone before.

The third synthesis, that of recognition, is the seeing of individual moments of experience as instances of a concept, as we recognize a particular shape on a page as a word having a certain meaning. Furthermore, recognition is the discerning, and sometimes the application, of the concept or principle which controls the relative ordering of the parts in a sequence of words, premises, numbers or physical actions. Thus, we recognize the meanings of individual words, and, knowing the syntax of the language, we begin to see the ideas which have determined the organization of the material we are reading. And still more actively, we often apply rules and formulae, as when in deriving series of numbers, mind registers the identity of the last number written (the synthesis of reproduction), and determines the next number that should be written, in accord with the order prescribed by a formula. Evidently, it is this third synthesis which is chiefly responsible for the intelligibility of experience; and I do not mean to disparage the importance on this score of the causal laws which determine that there shall be order in the objective world.

Taken together these three syntheses are both the heart of the Transcendental Deduction, and the source of a significant disagreement among Kant's readers. The point in dispute is his attitude toward the relation of the syntheses to consciousness. Kant describes his own analysis as "transcendental," meaning thereby that it is an account of the mental activities which produce coherence a priori in experience. On this view, experience is to be regarded as a sort of finished product, and the threefold synthesis is known inferentially as the condition for the unity of experience. However, there are places in the *Critique* where Kant argues that the unity of consciousness would be impossible if mind could not become conscious of the transcendental unity which conditions its empirical unity. Because they are the forms of activity of the transcendental unity, this would mean that it must be possible for us to become aware of the threefold synthesis.

We can put aside these questions of historical interpretation, concentrating instead upon the apparent fact that mind *is* frequently conscious of at least one of the syntheses. It may well be true that the unity of time and the activities of memory are only known inferentially by way of the experiences they make possible, but it is nevertheless true that there are many times when we are aware of applying a particular formula or rule. This is evident in cases where a hypothesis is adopted in order to impose order upon a range of experimental findings, and when moral injunctions are accepted as rules of conduct. Indeed, the conscious awareness of rules and principles is normally required in the early stages of mastering a technique, because it is crucial that the learner be made to discern the principles which determine why things are done as they are. Skilled practitioners are much less self-aware than are students, but even here, there is conscious attention to the rules when care is demanded, or merely when the actor is in a reflective mood. And last, at the opposite extreme from the student, where mental activities are highly sophisticated, reflexive awareness is again at a premium. Philosophers and mathematicians, for example, are often very much aware of applying a rule, step-by-step, until a conclusion is obtained. Though we must acknowledge that awareness of a rule is not a necessary condition for its application, examples like these show that there are crucial instances where the awareness of a rule is required. I stress this because, as we shall see, Wittgenstein denies that self-conscious adherence to a rule is ever a factor in its application.

IIIc. 2] We require a substantialist theory of mind to supplement Kant's description; (a) Argument for existence of nonintrospectable mental states; (b) Specificity and endurance of these states; (c) These states constitute the actuality of minds in the same way that such properties as mass constitute the actuality of physical objects; (d) The thesis that mind and body are identical.

Most of what Kant has to say about the threefold synthesis impresses me as being true, but at the same time, Kant's analysis of mind is incomplete. Emphasizing the activity of mind to the exclusion of other considerations, Kant implies that mind is pure act, and hence that mind is what it does. Whether or not Kant intends to say this, he is at least misleading for his failure to provide for the notion that mind is a substance.

In order to prove that this notion is required of every complete theory of mind, let us consider the example of two men who have studied a foreign language. They have attended the same lectures and spent exactly the same amount of time studying the lessons, but one of them finishes the course speaking the language while the other does not. Our problem is to account for this difference. A reference to the training they have received is of no help to us, because we have stipulated that this factor was constant. We also rule out any personal idiosyncrasy of the two men; we say, as is perfectly conceivable, that there were no distractions which prevented the man who has ultimately failed from concentrating on his lessons. In the end, when this and all similar explanations have been dismissed, we can only infer that one man reads, while the other does not, for the reason that the mind of the successful student has undergone a modification which may be described as the acquisition of a new mental state. Having this state is apparently a condition which must be satisfied if reading is to take place. One feature of the state is that people are unaware in any introspectionist sense that they have it. Rather than being a mood or conscious tone, this is a nonintrospectable mental state.

As I am regarding them, mental states of this kind are causal conditions for the production of our cognitive experiences. To say, as I have, that cognitive experiences like reading are constituted by the apprehending, reproducing and recognizing of a subject matter is to hold that these three syntheses are the modes of activity of a mind whose nonintrospectable mental states have been activated by a stimulus which has its origins in the external world, or in the mind itself. We may regard minds and physical objects as opposite poles, so that when cognitive experience is said to occur "between" these poles, the "between" will be understood as meaning that cognitive experience is an effect which is jointly produced by physical objects and by minds having nonintrospectable mental states.

This conception of mental activity squares with the model which has been our point of departure for the inference that substances, whether mental or physical, have dispositional properties. The interaction of physical objects with a mind having nonintrospectable mental states is a causal relationship, and the function of mental capacities is to qualify the mind to respond to its contacts with the world in the ways which Kant describes in his analysis of the threefold synthesis of the understanding.

I acknowledge that the greater part of this suggestion of mine is at variance with Kant's position. He says nothing about nonintrospectable mental states, and he denies, at least implicitly, that the threefold synthesis is an effect caused by the interaction of a mind with the world. Kant believes that there is no warrant for adopting either of these claims, because he holds that the category of causality only applies to the relations of sensuous intuitions. By limiting the range of application of this category, he aims to prevent us from giving a causal explanation for the occurrence of the threefold synthesis; the three syntheses determine what intelligibility our sensible experiences shall have, but they are not themselves sensible experiences, and so, the category of causality should not apply to them. This reminds us of the Kantian view that apprehension, reproduction and recognition are expressions of the spontaneous activity of the transcendental unity of apperception, and of Kant's belief that these syntheses are not caused, that they are not effects, and that they do not even occur in space and time. The existence of nonintrospectable mental states has only been determined on the assumption that these mental activities are caused. If they are not caused, we have no excuse for arguing that the occurrence of the threefold synthesis, as when someone reads, presupposes the existence of these mental states. We shall be forced to admit that the idea of mental substance is an unnecessary posit, and that mind is pure activity.

This view is acceptable to many people, but I feel no compunction in departing from it. Kant's position seems to me to be a dogmatic reaffirmation of the Cartesian dualism; it elaborates, but hardly enlarges upon an ontology which draws a categorical distinction between thought (transcendental apperception) and a realm of extended substances where causality is a significant factor. There is only one justification, however, for preferring this or any dualism to some variety of monism: there must be a conceptual difficulty which prevents us from applying the same categorical distinctions throughout all of being. But as it happens, there is no consideration of this kind supporting Kant's dualism. He merely stipulates that the category of causality should not be thought to apply beyond the range of sensible experience; failing to prove that it cannot apply beyond this range, Kant invites us to reject his stipulation. When this is done, we are free to apply the notion of causality to our analysis of mind, and to argue that the "transcendental" activities of mind are effects that are caused when minds having nonintrospectable mental states make contact with the world.

We turn now to the further characterization of these mental states. Unfortunately, and because of the method that is used to establish their existence, there is very little more that can be said about them. The inference that these states do exist is based upon a reference to the mental activity performed by the successful student in our example above, and so, I am only justified in saying as much about the mental states as is required to account for the occurrence of such activities. There seems in truth to be only one more aspect of these states which can be demonstrated by way of this method. This is the fact that mental states are specific in character. We are justified in saying this, because it is known that the man who has failed to learn the foreign language does speak his own language and does write his own name; and these are mental activities requiring possession of a mental state as a causal condition for their occurrence. If mental states are not specific, we should expect that the states which cause the man to speak his native language will be sufficient, in the presence of relevant supplementary conditions, to make him speak the foreign language as well, but evidently, this does not happen. We infer that the nonintrospectable mental states which are causal conditions for the man's speaking English are specific; and consequently, that any particular mental state will serve as a causal condition for only a special kind of mental effort.

One last claim I wish to make about mental states is that they endure when the mind is inactive. This is impossible to prove using the method which I have so far applied, because I have been talking about mental states by reference to the activities they causally condition, and I now want to make a claim about them which does not take this activity as its point of reference. A very ordinary, common-sense argument is helpful at this point. A man who has been taught to read, reads without further instruction each time that he takes up a book after the numerous lapses of time when his mind is not active in this way. It is reasonable to suppose that the mental state which causally conditions the activity of reading endures at times when a mind having the state is not reading. The alternative, and this is most unreasonable, is that the mind loses the mental state when it stops reading, then re-acquires it at the very time when it must have the state in order to read again.

Generally then, specificity and endurance are the properties which I am claiming for nonintrospectable mental states. Moreover, I want to say that mental states having these properties and serving as the factors whereby minds act as causal conditions, are the properties which at least partly constitute the actuality of minds. I add the modifying "partly," because it is conceivable that consciousness is also one of the constituent factors, rather than merely a symptom of the activity of mental states in the way that the glow of a copper wire is a symptom of the current passing through the wire.

It is relevant here to consider the possibility that the thesis proclaiming the identity of body and mind is correct. This is not an empirical hypothesis, because it equates factors like sensations and brain states which are empirically different. Let us suppose, however, that philosophers have constructed arguments which prove conclusively that mind and body are identical. Under those circumstances, there would be a convergence in the results of my philosophical conclusions about nonintrospectable mental states, and the physiologists' discovery of nerve-endings which must undergo some modification in order that, for example, people may read. Both the a priori and the empirical inquiries would then establish that mental states have existence, specificity and endurance. And furthermore, it would be possible for us to regard mental states as wholly constituting the actuality of minds in exactly the same way that gross physical properties, and, more fundamentally, atomic particles constitute the actuality of substances which are already acknowledged to be physical objects.

I recognize, of course, that no one has so far proved that minds and bodies are identical, and that my conclusions about mental activity and mental states must be defended independently of any reference to my belief that this is a valid theory. Moreover, Wittgenstein would never permit anyone to appeal to this theory on behalf of extrabehavioral considerations,[23] and I am exclusively concerned with his objections to these notions.

IIId. Wittgenstein's criticisms of unobservable mental activities and mental states, and replies to these criticisms.

Wittgenstein hammers away at the notion that mental activities such as reading are to be understood in terms of Kant's threefold synthesis and causally conditioning mental states. As I understand the relevant passages, he argues that the observer cannot determine through direct observation that the threefold synthesis occurs, or that nonintrospectable mental states are causal conditions for its occurrence, and so, having no other means of confirmation open to him, the observer is unable to validate claims that the mind works as Kant supposes because of having mental states. On the principle that something can be said to be the case only if there is direct evidence for it, Wittgenstein argues that activities like reading are in no way dependent upon the threefold synthesis and mental states.[24]

In order to put his case most forcefully, Wittgenstein uses mathematical examples, and talks of deriving series of numbers from algebraic formulae. His counter-argument is delivered in the context of a discussion over a student who has been instructed to interpret an algebraic formula in a certain way. The student has responded by writing out a series which has a definite orderliness to it, but which nonetheless is not the series which his instructor wanted him to write. The point at issue is to determine what the instructor should say of this effort; was the series derived systematically, or were the numbers merely written down at random? Wittgenstein cautions us that this question must be answered in light of the fact that ". . . there is no sharp distinction between a random mistake and a systematic one. That is, between what you are inclined to call 'random' and 'systematic.' "[25] This theme recurs in several paragraphs. In one of them Wittgenstein asks: "But where is the dividing line between this procedure (a complex, but apparently systematic derivation of a series from a formula) and a random one?"[26]

Wittgenstein's point, it seems, is that an observer learns to use the term "systematic" as a response to circumstances in which students write out series which instructors request them to derive. The observer, who is normally the instructor, knows how the student ought to respond in the circumstances, and he is befuddled when the response he sees is not the anticipated one. Responses which have a discernible orderliness to them cannot be described as random, and yet, relative to the circumstances, they are not properly systematic either. The difficulty becomes even more accentuated in cases such as the one where natives translate the rules of chess into rules for yelling and stamping their feet.[27] Observers who are only familiar with the ordinary board-game would be completely at a loss if they saw chess being played in this way. The rules for using "systematic" and "random" would completely break down, and the observers would be free to use whichever expression they preferred in describing the natives' behavior.

Wittgenstein has adopted a highly subjective interpretation of what is systematic or random, and, as before, he has done so because the observer of overt behavior has difficulties in verifying what the subject of observation has actually done. This interpretation strikes me as being no less objectionable than the claim that it is meaningless to say that a rule has been obeyed when someone makes a single correct utterance or report. We have to save a linguistic distinction, reflecting an objective difference in matters of fact, from ambiguity, just as we previously had to save entire statements from meaninglessness. Because of our discussion of Kant's syntheses, the required distinction can be sharply redrawn. And in this way: the synthesis of recognition was described as the activity by which a schema that may be a philosophical idea or an algebraic formula determines the order in which premises of an argument, or the numbers of a series are written out. The question of whether or not this synthesis occurs is concerned with an objective matter of fact. The idea or formula has controlled the derivation or it has not; if it has, the argument or series is systematic, and if not, it is random. In practice, it may be impossible to tell whether a series is random or systematic, as when people jot down series of marks on the edges of their newspapers, but are unable to tell us whether a formula was applied when we call their attention to the figures. The observer does not know what to say in cases like these, but the series do, nonetheless, have a history; they were systematically derived from formulae or they were not, and the observer is not free to say what he likes.

Wittgenstein himself anticipates and replies to this objection as follows:

> Has he understood the system when he continues the series to the hundredth place? . . . Perhaps you will say here; to have got the system (or again to understand it) can't consist in continuing the series up to this or that number; that is only applying one's understanding. The understanding itself is a state which is the source of the correct use . . . Isn't one thinking of the derivation of a series from its algebraic formula . . . The point is, we can think of more than one application of an algebraic formula; and every type of application can in turn be formulated algebraically; but naturally this does not get us any further. . . . The application is still a criterion of understanding.[28]

Wittgenstein responds to theories of mental activity like the one I am proposing by interpreting them to claim that derivation of a series from its algebraic formula is the point at issue, and this, I believe, reveals why it is that Wittgenstein prefers to make his counter-argument by way of mathematical examples. Wittgenstein is about to reject the rationalist theory of mind *on account of the difficulties that an observer has in applying algebraic formulae to descriptions of overt behavior.* There would be no equivalent vehicle for this counter-argument if reading were the example, because a mental state attributed to people who read could not plausibly be described as an algebraic formula, and reading could not be said to be a derivation from it. The idea of a formula from which series are derived is however at least vaguely similar to the idea of a mental state causally conditioning a mental activity, and so mathematical examples make it slightly less incongruous when Wittgenstein begins by supposing that mental states which causally condition the use of algebraic formulae are themselves just those formulae, and that Kant's syntheses are merely derivations of numbers from formulae. It is clear that Wittgenstein's interpretation of the rationalist theory is entirely alien to the views of people who talk about mental activity and mental states as I have done, and that his representation of the faculty theory prejudices the coming arguments in his own favor.

The above quotation shows that Wittgenstein has two criticisms of the faculty theory. First, there is the statement that ". . . we can think of more than one application of an algebraic formula." This is a cryptic response, but perhaps Wittgenstein is saying that we ought not to hypothesize that there are mental states conditioning the derivation of series from formulae, because the state might condition the derivation of various series. The upshot of this criticism will then be that rationalist explanations of how we derive series are incomplete. If one mental state is the condition for the derivation of many series, Wittgenstein can ask why it is that one series rather than another is derived. The existence of the mental state is presumably inferred in order to account for the deriving of a particular series, but if it turns out that the mental state is not sufficient to account for the derivation, we will have to suppose that there is still another mental state operative. This last mental state might again be the condition for deriving a variety of series, and we would have the makings of an infinite regress.

Supporting this interpretation of Wittgenstein's point is the retort he makes in another paragraph:

"But how can a rule show me what I have to do at this point? Whatever I do is, on some interpretation, in accord with the rule." — This is not what we ought to say, but rather: any interpretation still hangs in the air along with what it interprets, and cannot give it any support. Interpretations by themselves do not determine meaning.[29]

The point of the first line of this passage is dismissed in favor of the one made in the following lines, as Wittgenstein leads back to the view that mental activity is only a matter of responding correctly to particular circumstances. At the same time, this first line embodies an argument which Wittgenstein directs at opponents of his behaviorism; having stunned them with the argument he returns to his own position.

The argument of the first line appears to be the one which Wittgenstein is developing against positions like my own. The mental state is thought to be a formula which can be applied in several ways, and the intimation is that people like myself must retreat one step, and hypothesize a state to account for every kind of derivation made from the original formula. Wittgenstein can then say that each of these states is also an algebraic formula, and can be applied in making several derivations. He will then have all that is required to charge us with inviting an infinite regress.

The reply to this criticism is that Wittgenstein is arguing against a misconstruction of the rationalist theory: Wittgenstein, but none of us, has said that the mental state is to be regarded as a formula. It is true that a formula may be interpreted in several ways, but this does not mean that a mental state is the condition for deriving more than a single series. If the mental state is not regarded as a formula, and if each mental state conditions the derivation of only one series, there is no threat of an infinite regress; and Wittgenstein's argument can be rejected for being wide of the mark.

In his second counter-argument, Wittgenstein objects that ". . . every type of application can in turn be formulated algebraically." This remark has to be taken in conjunction with the last line of the paragraph in which it appears. That reads: "The application is still a criterion of understanding." Someone is being reassured that he still has the behavioral criterion for distinguishing systematically derived series

from random ones. The suggestion is that the rationalists'
criterion is no longer available. It must be the observer who
is being reassured; he is the one who will apply the behaviorist criterion, and the problem is to determine why the
rationalists' criterion is not good enough for him.

With this interpretation of the background, the structure of Wittgenstein's argument stands out more sharply.
The observer is the man who is objecting that every series is
algebraically formulable. Any sequence of marks produced by
a student looks to him as if it might have been systematically
derived, because he can always imagine that the student has
used the formula which the observer himself conceives while
taking notes on the student's progress. The observer is never
assured that he is not overinterpreting the situation; the
learner may not be applying any formula at all, and his figures
may be no more than a random scrawl. The observer is suffering one of his frequent embarrassments, and he objects,
because he prefers to avoid them in the future.

Though Wittgenstein does not allude to it in the passage quoted above, there is a further difficulty. Any series can
be formulated in a number of ways, and supposing that the
student has used a formula in working out a series, the observer will not be able to tell which of several of them the
student has used.

As it appears then, Wittgenstein's general conclusion is
that the rationalists' suggestion would, if true, be a frequent
source of difficulty for the observer. He is unable to tell
whether any formula is being used, or if so, which one is. The
observer could only protect himself if he had direct access to
the learner's mental processes, but for want of that, overt
behavior is his only guide. Consequently, the rationalists'
criterion for distinguishing systematically derived series is useless in practice, and ought to be rejected.

As it stands, Wittgenstein's argument is not quite to
the point, because it supposes, as before, that mental states
are algebraic formulae. Before assessing the argument, let us
suppose, contrary to fact, that Wittgenstein acknowledges the

difference between formulae and mental states, and let us assume also that he admits that the application of a formula is causally conditioned by a mental state. The argument will then be that our inability to determine whether or not anyone is using a formula disables us from ever knowing whether a mental state has conditioned his behavior. The conclusion will be the same as before: the rationalist criterion is unsatisfactory, because the observer cannot use it to identify systematically derived series.

Two things can be said in response to this criticism. First, rationalist faculty psychologists are not worried about the observer. In this particular case, a reference to Kant's synthesis of recognition has been introduced in order to save a distinction from the subjectivity into which Wittgenstein has let it fall. Wittgenstein has ultimately left it up to the observer to decide whether a series has been systematically derived or is only a random collection of marks, and I have argued, in response, that a more objective standard is required. Admittedly, an observer cannot tell by way of direct observation of a man's behavior, whether a concept or a formula is being applied, but this has not been the fundamental consideration. Rather than to accommodate the observer-centered view, the purpose has been to supplement it.

A second response to Wittgenstein's argument is that the notion of applying a concept or rule is not so useless for the observer as it is made out to be. The observer is to suppose that a series either has or has not been derived by mind from a formula, and this should help him to direct his inquiries. Wittgenstein, moreover, exaggerates the difficulties which observers have in applying the criterion. Someone might spend all of his time trying to confuse his friends with aberrant interpretations of familiar formulae, but this is surely uncommon. Awareness of the circumstances, knowledge of a man's training, and our own ability are of some help in determining whether a formula is being used. If these are not sufficient, we can usually ask the man how he has worked out the series or the argument. Once we discover that a formula has been used, we can infer, though Wittgenstein denies it, that a nonintrospectable mental state has conditioned its application.

Wittgenstein's counter-arguments have so far accepted the possibility that series might be derived from formulae, but now, thinking that he has refuted even this watered-down version of the rationalist view, Wittgenstein withdraws into his behaviorism, and closes the door tightly against further rationalist intrusions. This finishing touch makes it seem as though rationalist descriptions of mental activity are misconceived solutions to an illusory problem. He writes:

> This was our paradox: no course of action could be determined by a rule, because every course of action can be made out to accord with the rule. The answer was: if everything can be made out to accord with the rule, then it can also be made out to conflict with it. And so there would be neither accord nor conflict here. It can be seen that there is a misunderstanding here from the mere fact that in the course of our argument we give one interpretation after another; as if each one contented us at least for a moment, until we thought of yet another standing behind it. What this shows is that there is a way of grasping a rule which is *not* an *interpretation*, but which is exhibited in what we call "obeying the rule" and "going against it" in actual cases.[30]

The paradox is generated by the second of the two counter-arguments which were considered above. An observer who adopts the rationalist criterion for distinguishing systematically derived series will try to imagine the formula that a man is using for the derivation of a particular series. When he conceives of a likely formula, the observer predicts the next addition that should be made to the series, but he errs as the development of the series deviates sharply from what he has anticipated. The observer tries to keep up by modifying his interpretation of the first rule he has conceived, or by thinking up an entirely new rule; but each time, after perhaps one, or even many correct predictions, the rule disappoints him, as the series takes an unexpected turn. These appear to be the shifts of interpretation which Wittgenstein regards as a clue that the whole enterprise is misconceived. It is mistaken to suppose that a man is using a rule to direct his activities, because no-one ever uses a rule for this purpose.

Rationalists think otherwise, because they have fallen into an observer's trap. Of course, the rationalist, himself, is merely an observer, and he emphasizes conceptual rules, as observers typically do, because the rules help him to see experience in ordered patterns. But the rationalist is mistaken to suppose that people who are observed use these rules to dictate the sequence of their own actions. He only thinks that they do, because he fails to notice that there are conflicting interpretations of the formulae which he uses to predict their actions, and then imputes to them as rules guiding their conduct. These same formulae may be interpreted in ways that make conduct look disordered and random, or systematic and rational. Indeed, the rationalist's claim about how others think is now clearly revealed as nothing more than a reflection of the way that he thinks about them. This is not to say that people try to be random and disorganized in their behavior. This imputation is no more warranted than the rationalist one, for both claims are symptoms of the same misguided attempt to force our idea of mental activity into a traditional conception of how we think minds ought to perform. We want to say that rational beings naturally do use rules, and that people who are not using them must be trying not to. But this picture is mistaken, and the categories native to it are irrelevant. Descriptions of mental activity should concentrate upon particular circumstances, and the blind, mechanical responses which they provoke.[31]

The last, and psychologistic, half of this argument is largely imaginative reconstruction on my part, but these additions appear to be consistent with Wittgenstein's thinking. The argument reveals how important it was for Wittgenstein to respond to the rationalist description of mental activity by saying that this must be the notion that series are derived from algebraic formulae. Formulae may be interpreted so that they accord or conflict with empirical data, but mental states cannot be so regarded. Let us assume, however, that mental states are merely algebraic formulae. Does this help Wittgenstein to prove that an observer's ability to regard action in ways that accord and conflict with a rule entails that rules are never used to fix the direction of human behavior?

There can be no doubt that his is a bad argument. Imagine the huckster at a carnival who offers prizes if he fails to guess your weight correctly. It is a cold day, and volunteers are warmly dressed; so cold in fact that they resist the expert's invitation to remove their overcoats. This makes it very awkward for the carnival man, because he doesn't know what to make of the bulge in a side pocket. However, being an expert, he accepts the first ten volunteers; and only after they walk away with ten of his prizes does the inspiration come to him. He will prepare a great sign: "This is a weight-guessing game. It is not open to people wearing overcoats, because they weigh nothing at all." The logic of Wittgenstein's argument brings him to a similar conclusion. The observer is at a disadvantage, and therefore, we are to eliminate the source of his confusion. But surely this is unreasonable; there are matters of fact and attempts to discover them, and the annihilation of the one is not entailed by mere observational difficulties in the other. It is true enough that observers are often at a disadvantage, but who, other than Wittgenstein, cares to deny that mathematicians, architects, and, indeed, all of us, regularly apply formulae, plans, and ideas in deciding what our actions shall be? What man acknowledging the reality of these often self-conscious mental activities will want to deny that the activities are caused, that the mind is one of the causal conditions, and that it functions as a cause by way of states which are comparable if not identical with brain states?

Though he never explicitly says this, I think that Wittgenstein would have us believe that his conclusions do follow, if we accept an observer-centered view of mental activity. In that event, the absence of empirical criteria for determining that a formula was used will be the critical point, because empirical data will be the observer's only source of information, and because a statement whose truth cannot in principle be determined by direct observation will not be open to confirmation. The traditional empiricist conclusion will then follow: a statement that could never be confirmed will not be meaningful. On that assumption, it would now be fair to ask how we came to believe that people sometimes use rules or formulae to determine the sequence of their actions, and a psychological explanation of the sort I interpolated into Wittgenstein's argument would be in order.

All of this fails, however, to answer the prior question of why we should suppose that an observer-centered theory of mind is the only legitimate one. Wittgenstein never tells us why he thinks that it is, and yet he meets every criticism of his behaviorist theory with the implicit assumption that the criticism cannot be made, because it violates strict empiricist requirements. Perhaps there are others, but I can think of only two justifications for this approach. First, Wittgenstein might have established that empiricist assumptions are the only reasonable ones to apply in a study of mind. Because he has failed to do this, the burden of proof shifts to the other possibility. It must be demonstrated that an empiricist, behaviorist, account of mental activity is sufficient to describe and explain all dimensions of mental life. The foregoing arguments have been intended to show that behaviorism is not sufficient.

A modest example, one already mentioned above, proves that behaviorism cannot explain even simple differences in human conduct. Two students go through the same training, but in the end only one of them is able to perform. Wittgenstein has argued that particular circumstances prompt a man who has received a special training to respond in an appropriate manner, but evidently training and reproduction of the relevant circumstances are not enough. Something is missing when a man who has undergone training fails to respond. To account for the fact that a competitor is successful, we have to make a simple inference; we suppose that this man has acquired a certain mental state, and we say that this state was the missing causal condition when the first man stood up to the circumstances and failed to respond. Far from being an exhaustive theory of mind, it turns out that behaviorism describes the evidence, but leaves it for other theories to provide the explanations.

This is evidence, enough I think, for saying that Wittgenstein's exclusively behaviorist theory of mind is unsatisfactory; and for our purposes, that nonintrospectable mental states do exist.

4

REAL POTENTIALITY

Having settled the question of whether mental states exist, we have all the distinctions that are required for a final characterization of dispositional properties. Dispositions have so far been described as the potentialities which qualify minds and objects to participate in causal relationships, and analysis in this chapter will center upon the argument by which Aristotle proves the irreducibility of potentiality to actuality. I shall develop the implications of this argument, and of certain other passages in which Aristotle enlarges upon his conception of potentiality.

IVa. Aristotle's suggestion that we use indirect means to discover characteristics of potentiality; B. *Possible indirect methods of analysis;* 1] *The advantages and disadvantages of an ordinary language analysis;* 2] *The reductio ad absurdum;* 3] *Criticisms of the reductio by ordinary language philosophers;* 4] *Responses to those criticisms.*

Aristotle would have us direct our analysis as follows:

Actuality, then, is the existence of a thing not in the way which we express by "potentially"; we say that potentially, for instance, a statue of Hermes is in the block of wood and the half-line is in the whole, because it might be separated out, and we call even the man who is not studying a man of science, if he is capable of studying; the thing that stands in contrast to each of these exists actually. Our meaning can be seen in the particular cases by induction, and we must not seek a definition of everything but be content to grasp the analogy, that it is as that which is building is to that which is capable of building, and the waking to that which has its eyes shut but has sight, and that which has been shaped out of the matter to the matter, and that which has been wrought up to the unwrought. Let actuality be defined by one member of this antithesis, and the potential by the other. But all things are not said in the same sense to exist actually, but only by analogy — as A is in B or to B, C is in D or to D; for some are as movement to potency and the others as substance to some sort of matter.[1]

Two problems are distinguished in this paragraph, and only one of them concerns us now. Our problem is described, in the last line of the passage, as the relation of "movement to potency." Aristotle, however, has opened *Metaphysics* IX with notice that he is primarily concerned with another issue:

And first let us explain potency in the strictest sense, which is however, not the most useful for our present purpose. For potency and actuality extend beyond the cases that involve a reference to motion. But when we have spoken of this first kind, we shall in our discussion of actuality explain the other kinds of potency as well.[2]

The potentiality that is most usefully discussed in Book Nine is the potentiality of relatively unformed matter to become better formed. This discussion is occupied with the set of problems referred to in the last line of the first quotation above as the relation of "substance to matter." In the preceding books of the *Metaphysics*, Aristotle has stressed the analysis of single substances rather than the analysis of the dynamic relations of substances, and the argument has been that substances are constituted of form and matter. In Book Nine this discussion undergoes a shift in language as form comes to be described as actuality and matter is described as potentiality; matter is said to have a potency for becoming informed.

The crucial difference between these two ways of regarding potentiality is that discussion of the evolution of form in a single substance makes no reference to the circumstances in which successive developmental changes occur, while potentialities "in the strictest sense" are the properties which make it possible for objects to suffer modifications of their form when they interact with other substances. Aristotle apparently deviates from his analysis in order to mention the notion of potentiality which concerns us, because the potency of matter to become better formed must ultimately be described as the power of a substance to undergo change when it is acted upon by other things. For this reason, we may continue to devote ourselves to this latter sort of potentiality without fearing that we have overlooked an equally primitive though different potency.

The first notable assertion which Aristotle has made about potentiality is that we cannot have a definition for it. His reason for saying this is a belief that definitions are by genus and differentia, and the problem here is that philosophy ". . . deals with terms that are not included within any one genus but are common to all being as such."[3] Potentiality is one of the categorical, philosophic notions, and consequently, it cannot be defined.

This explains Aristotle's motive for prescribing an indirect, rather than direct, approach to the nature of potentiality; recall that he mentions analogy as an example of this method. The direct and scientific method of analysis would be to deduce a conclusion giving the genus and specific difference of potentiality from major and minor premises, but this method is useless to us, because potentiality does not have a genus and specific difference. Potentiality is a mode of being, but being is not a genus. Consequently, we must apply special techniques of indirect argument if the nature of potentiality is to be clarified.

Aristotle has advised us to begin the analysis by considering actual states of affairs. The reason for adopting this particular indirect approach is that our understanding of potentiality is parasitic upon our understanding of what it is to be an actuality. Another way to put this is to say, with Aristotle, that actuality ". . . is prior in formula"[4] to potentiality, or that we cannot know that things of one kind have a potentiality until some one of them shows us that it does by suffering or effecting a change. What it shows us, of course, is an actual state of affairs, and we subsequently infer that anything which did act in this way must have had the potentiality to do so. It is in this way that actuality is prior to potentiality in knowledge, and it is for this reason that claims about the nature of potentiality begin by acknowledging that causal conditions have produced certain changes.

A cautionary note is in order; we will avoid possible confusion by keeping several distinctions in mind. The actuality that is prior to potentiality in knowledge is the actuality that *succeeds* potentiality in time. The potentiality for building, possessed by any single man, is prior in time to the act of building. However, we only know that he has the potentiality when we see him actively building; after seeing him perform in this way, we look back and say that he must have had the potentiality to build in order to have acted as he has done. The order of our knowledge is just the opposite from the temporal order in which a thing first comes to have a potentiality, and then produces a change. This becomes further complicated. Shortly below, the priority of actuality in being will be introduced. This is a different actuality from the actuality prior in knowledge. The change produced is the actuality that is prior in knowledge, but it is the man who has potentiality for producing the change who is prior in being. The priority of this actuality to its potentiality is logical rather than temporal. These distinctions may be obscure, but further discussion should help to clarify them.

Returning to the argument, our first problem is to decide how to approach the actuals prior in knowledge to potentiality. We could examine our perceptions, but this is unlikely to be a fruitful start, because objects of perception are necessarily actuals, and having little sophistication at this point, we wouldn't know how to analyze the actuals for clues that would lead us to the corresponding potentialities.

It is easier to begin by examining certain terms and phrases in ordinary language. For every term or phrase referring to an actual state of affairs, language provides another expression, or a rule for constructing one, which refers to a corresponding potentiality. If we survey pairs of these expressions, we are likely to find the element that is common to them. We begin by considering the terms which refer to the potentialities, and we hope to discover what their meanings intimate about the relation between the potentialities to which they refer, and the actualities referred to by the other terms of the several pairs. If we take the expressions "that which is building" and "that which can build" as our examples, we find that language prevents us from saying that a man is building but that he cannot build. This is generally the case, for it is never proper to say that an effect has been suffered or initiated, unless we can also say that the substance acting as a causal condition has or had the capacity to perform in this way. Language would have us conclude that things must be able to perform as causal conditions as a condition for actually being them and producing effects.

This conceptual analysis is effective enough for a start, but it can never be more than the preliminary to a metaphysical argument, because we require a method which will enable us to substantiate the claims which conceptual analysis would have us make about the world. Harking back to Aristotle's example, we have to ascertain that the capacity for building is *in fact* a condition for the effort of building.

The method for establishing this is the *reductio ad absurdum*. Arguments of this form step outside of language and make contact with the world by virtue of the fact that their first premises are assertions that some aspect of the world is as we undeniably discover it to be. We apply a *reductio* in order to test the claim that there is a factor related to this given aspect as a condition for its being as it is. We prove that our claim is valid by denying that it is, and by drawing out the implications of this second premise of the *reductio*. When it has been demonstrated that this premise is in conflict with the first one, we reject it in favor of its affirmative opposite, and we say that the factor in question is a condition for events being as we have described them in the first premise. Two considerations are thus established; first, we prove that the aspect accepted as given would not be as it is, if this factor were not conditioning it, and second, by considering its function relative to the given aspect, we establish the reality of this factor.

Conceptual analysts frequently take exception to the view that a *reductio* can provide information about the world. They remind us that an argument of this form uses expressions which are borrowed from ordinary language, and they insist that the argument amounts to a conceptual analysis whose aim is to expose the entailments to which we are committed when we utter the second premise of the argument in ordinary speech. Consequently, the objection goes, denying the second premise is merely a way of indicating that ordinary language does not permit us to talk consistently if we assert both the first and the second premises. This, however, is thought to be a proof of logical conflicts in language, rather than a source of information about matters of fact.

This response, as it seems to me, fails to distinguish the essentially passive and non-philosophic activity of cataloguing the rules of linguistic usage, from the philosophic method of actively refining concepts until they provide for the salient categorical distinctions of facts in being. Thus, a philosopher who shows us the implications of the second premise of a *reductio* has not merely fastened upon an argument which he could have accepted unquestioningly from an encyclopedia of linguistic usage. To the contrary, his efforts to construct an adequate philosophic concept have brought him to a point where he understands that there are only two possible combinations of categorical distinctions in being, and his *reductio* has the force of eliminating one of these possibilities. It may be the case that ordinary language provides for the distinction whose reality has now been established, but this is not surprising when we recall that language is a practical tool for communicating about the world, and that it is a useful tool just to the extent that it provides for a large number of the categorical distinctions which prevail in being.

If we compare the two methods, we find that a *reductio* has two great advantages over the analysis of ordinary language-expressions. First, it brings us into contact with the world by taking some matter of fact as its point of reference. Second, the *reductio* admits no claim in explanation of this matter of fact, unless it can be demonstrated that the fact would not be as it is, if the distinction did not obtain. This is a control upon the number of categorical distinctions which can be adduced in accounting for the matter of fact which has been accepted as given. By comparison, linguistic analysis makes no contact with the world, except unpredictably and unconsciously as the distinctions which it draws happen to reflect distinctions in being. Furthermore, ordinary language analysis is unrestrained by considerations of economy. The conceptual analyst is likely to feel that he has done an incomplete job, unless he reports every nuance which is characteristic of the rules for using an expression. He has no way of telling, from within language, how many of these nuances represent distinctions which have an independent standing in being. And this, of course, reflects the disadvantage of making no contact with the world. For both of these reasons, we are justified in saying that the *reductio ad absurdum* supersedes conceptual analysis as the method for determining the nature of potentiality.

IVc. *Aristotle's* reductio: *potentiality is not reducible to actuality;* 1] *The Megarians;* 2] *First half of Aristotle's argument;* 3] *W. D. Ross's criticism;* 4] *Aristotle's conclusion;* (a) *Potentiality not reducible to actuality which is prior to potentiality in knowledge;* (b) *Supplementary arguments: potentiality is not reducible to actuality which is prior to potentiality in being.*

Aristotle was fully aware of the advantages of the *reductio*, and he applies one in order to prove that having a potentiality is a condition for producing an effect. Aristotle directs his argument against the Megarian conclusion that

> A thing "can" act only when it is acting, and when it is not acting it "cannot" act, e.g., that he who is not building cannot build, but only he who is building, when he is building; and so on in all other cases.[5]

This view is already familiar to us as the position of philosophers who analyze "can" statements as "shall-if" statements. It holds that potentiality is reducible to the actuality which is prior to potentiality in knowledge.

The Megarians argued in this way, because they held the distorted notion that a potentiality for initiating or suffering change is a kind of quasi-actuality. Their argument was that a man who has the potentiality for standing while he is sitting will truly be said to be both sitting and standing; but that obviously a man cannot be both sitting and standing, so that the potentiality for standing cannot be different from the actual fact of standing.

Aristotle responds to this argument without correcting its mistaken assumption. He merely points out that failure to distinguish what is done from what can be done has disastrous consequences for the fact that causal conditions produce changes. Change is an obvious point of reference for Aristotle's counter-argument, because he has already defined movement, a kind of change, as ". . . the fulfillment of what exists potentially,"[6] or in alternative translation, as ". . . the actualization of the potential qua potential." The point of the counter-argument is that the Megarian view entails that causes should be incapable of producing effects, for as Aristotle writes:

> If that which is deprived of potency is incapable, that which is not happening will be incapable of happening; but he who says of that which is incapable of happening either that it is or that it will be will say what is untrue: for this is what incapacity meant. Therefore their views do away with both movement and becoming. For that which stands will always stand, and that which sits will always sit, since if it is sitting it will not get up; for that which, as we are told, cannot get up will be incapable of getting up.[7]

In essence, the claim which Aristotle makes is that substances would not interact with one another, and thereby produce specific effects, if they did not have potentialities qualifying them to interact as they do. This is only the negative side of Aristotle's argument, but it is well to evaluate this part, before going on to his positive conclusion.

There seems to me to be no way in which the argument could be improved, but W. D. Ross is not impressed. As he sees it:

> This last argument appears to be fallacious. The real meaning of the Megarian doctrine seems to be that there is no such thing as capacity or possibility. A thing either is happening or it is not happening, and that is all that there is to be said about it. Therefore of that which is not happening they would say, not that it is incapable of happening; but that there is no sense in saying that it is capable of happening; and this does not imply a denial of change — it would be compatible with the assertion that change exists but is always necessary.[8]

His argument takes its first turning, when Ross claims that

"the Megarian doctrine seems to be that there is no such thing as capacity or possibility." As the subsequent steps make clear, Ross conceives "capacity" and "possibility" as synonyms. Consequently, when Aristotle shows the absurdities to which one is led by denying that things have a capacity for change, Ross interprets him as proving only that difficulties follow if we deny that there is possible change. Ross then argues that necessary change is not covered by Aristotle's *reductio*.

I suggest that this is a misconstruction of Aristotle's argument, and that the original error is to hold that "capacity," as used by Aristotle, and "possibility," as used by Ross are synonyms. It is true that "capacity" or "potentiality," and "possibility" frequently have the same meaning, but they would not be synonymous if Aristotle's argument were expanded so as to require the use of both "possibility" and "potentiality."

As preliminary to outlining the expanded argument, we have to consider the meanings of "possibility" and "necessity." As Ross is using "possibility," it apparently means "that which might occur." Changes that might occur are those which would not be exceptions to the principle of contradiction, or in violation of physical law; but in addition, a possible change is one that could occur, because the conditions for its happening are available, though they are not assembled. Thus, one sort of change is possible if we have access to dry wood, oxygen, and a heat source. These are causal conditions, and on occasions where all of them and other supplementary conditions are present, and where nothing like a cloudburst intervenes, the wood must burn. Here, and consistently with Ross's usage, "necessity" means "that which must occur when causal conditions are fulfilled." When "possibility" and "necessity" are conceived in this way, we see that *all* change is necessary. Possible change is not change, but only the prospect that change might occur.

These definitions of "possible" and "necessary" may be no more than approximations of what Aristotle means by the terms. Still, the approximations help to distinguish possible and necessary change from potentiality, and to show that potentiality is logically prior to both possible and necessary change. Aristotle's point is that substances must have potentialities in order to participate in causal relationships. Change would not be possible if there were no substances endowed with the potentialities for producing it; and for want of the things that could change and be changed, nothing would suffer alteration by way of interaction with other substances.

Having successfully, I think, demonstrated the absurdity of the Megarian position, Aristotle dismisses their view and substitutes his own:

> But we cannot say this [that the sitting man cannot stand, when *ex hypothesi* he is standing], so that evidently potency and actuality are different (but these views make potency and actuality the same, and so it is no small thing they are seeking to annihilate), so that it is possible that a thing may be capable of being and not be, and capable of not being and yet be, and similarly with the other kinds of predicate; it may be capable of walking and yet not walk, or capable of not walking and yet walk.[9]

This is the final stroke to an invulnerable argument. Aristotle begins by acknowledging that substances produce effects, and he invites us to deny that substances have powers before the effects are produced. Evidently, however, this cannot be denied, because it means that things will be incapable of producing effects, and entails that it should be impossible for the effects to occur. There is no denying that changes do occur, and hence, the belief that things can act only when they do act must be mistaken. The potentiality for producing a change cannot be reducible to the state of affairs in which the change is produced.

By establishing this point, Aristotle meets one of the two objections to be overcome if we are to prove that potentiality is real. He demonstrates that potentiality is not reducible to the actuality which is prior to potency in knowledge, and only leaves it for us to show here that potentiality cannot be reduced to the actuality which is prior in being. The full meaning of this phrase *prior in being* is not to be elucidated for some pages yet, but it is already clear enough for us to recognize that this second required proof for the irreducibility of potentiality has been provided in the first chapter of this book. We imagined a world in which objects are identical to substances of our world in respect to all properties which determine how they shall exist as actuals, but where the changes produced by these objects are different from the ones produced by apparently identical objects in our world. Having already argued that dispositions are properties qualifying things to be causal conditions, we inferred that things causing different effects must have different powers. The conclusion of the argument then followed: if the powers are different while properties constituting the actuality of the objects are the same, the powers cannot be reducible to properties like shape and mass; not being reducible to these properties, they must be real potentialities.

I believe that this argument is conclusive, but to place the issue even further beyond doubt, we can modify Aristotle's *reductio* so that it too will prove that there is a difference between potentialities and the properties which constitute the actuality of substances. Our first premise acknowledges that changes are produced by sets of causal conditions, and also as before, we say that a man who was sitting is now standing. Our second premise is that the capacity for standing is reducible to factors like the posture of a man's bones when he is in a sitting position. Now seeking to expose the implications of this premise, we begin by asking for an interpretation of what "reducible" means in this case. Unavoidably, I think, we regard it as signifying that "the capacity for standing" is a misleading phrase which appears to refer to an occult power, despite the fact that it only refers to the actual condition of a body which is sitting. But now consider: a man who has no capacity for standing should remain sitting for all time. Remembering that this contradicts our first premise, we have to deny the premise which entails this conclusion, and to reaffirm the view that powers are irreducible to the properties which constitute the actuality of things. For want of another alternative, this means that powers are real potentialities.

This, as it seems to me, is a second proof for the irreducibility of potentiality to the actuality of minds and objects, and by settling this point we are justified in turning to the major problem which faces a realist theory of dispositions after the arguments of the first chapter.

IVc. 5] Four features of potentiality proved or implied by Aristotle's reductio; (a) Potentiality is a logical condition for the production of change; (b) Potentiality is not reducible to actuality; (c) Potentialities are specific; (d) Potentialities are the properties of minds and objects.

Even though it is true that there cannot be a definition of potentiality, we are obliged to give some information about its characteristics, and, most of all, to give an accounting of the relation holding between real potentialities and the properties which constitute the actuality of minds and objects. This is the great merit of Aristotle's refutation of the Megarians; it proves or at any rate implies four significant claims about potentiality:

1]   Aristotle proves that potentiality is a necessary condition for the production of change by showing that effects would not be produced if substances did not have potentialities to qualify them for participation in causal relationships. This is the key to subsequent discussion, for having determined what potentiality does, we can use this as our point of reference in establishing what it is.

2]   The second claim, and, as I have said, this is only partly established by Aristotle's *reductio*, is that potentiality is an irreducible mode of being. The interaction of minds and objects would not produce effects, if these substances did not have real potentialities. This is our first information about the nature of potentiality, though as it happens, this only tells us that potentiality is not identical with actuality, and, therefore, that it cannot be described in any of the terms used to characterize actuality qua actuality. This means that potentialities are not any kind of substance or event.

3]   Potentialities are specific. In refusing to define potentiality, Aristotle has said, "Our meaning can be seen in particular cases by induction," and he has gone on to refer to the various potentialities which condition the production of specific changes. Similarly, his argument against the Megarians refers to specific potentialities for sitting and standing. This third point is one of the assumptions about potentiality which Aristotle makes but never proves, and an argument for it will have to be provided. The argument will hold that potentialities could not be conditions for the production of effects, and that, consequently, effects could not be produced, if potentialities were not specific.

4]   Another implicit assumption in Aristotle's *reductio* is that potentialities belong to minds and objects. He argues that effects would not be produced, unless there were capacities for producing them prior to the time when the effects occur; and, he assumes that these capacities pertain to the minds and objects which act as causal conditions. This is a reasonable view to take when one considers the fact to be accounted for, and the available solutions. The problem is to locate potentialities in order to show how they can be conditions for change, and there appear to be just two possible ways of doing this: we can either say that potentialities are the properties of substances, or that there is a force in the world which always introduces potentialities into sets of causal conditions when powers are required for the production of a change. Certainly this occasionalist doctrine is much less promising than the assumption which Aristotle makes. I shall try to prove that Aristotle has made the right choice by isolating the factors in minds and objects which are responsible for their having powers.

These are the four characteristics which emerge when the fact that causes produce effects is taken as the point of departure for the analysis of potentiality. Other claims made about dispositions (as, for example, that they endure) cannot be supported unless these four points, and especially the last one, are acknowledged. It may be that potentiality has other characteristics which can be determined by arguing backwards from the fact of change to the features of the conditioning potentialities, but I am unable to discover them.

There is one familiar, and previously unmentioned, conception of potentiality which appears to have a bearing upon change, but I have neglected this conception because it strikes me as being misconceived. This is the view that some things are active causal agencies while others are passive, on account of having powers which are respectively active and passive. Another version of this is the idea that some powers well up and force actualization, though others are recessive or nearly inert and require stimulation before the object having them can respond. The hazard in these notions is that the distinction between activity and passivity is first made in talking of actual occurrences, and that we chance making an unnecessary claim about potentiality, unless we can prove that this distinction is required in accounting for the manner in which potentiality conditions change; in itself, metaphorical application of the phrase does not establish anything about potentialities as they are in being.

As it happens, no proof is forthcoming, because we do not require this distinction in accounting for the fact that causes produce effects. It is enough to say that a thing which is active or passive has a power to act in that way. There is no reason to add that the power is itself active or passive. If we say, for example, that a man is self-controlled, we do not mean that his capacity for being agitated has to be prodded before he loses control. The capacity is neither active nor passive, though it is a power to be active, and the man will respond as it qualifies him to do when certain causal conditions are fulfilled. This is reason enough, I think, for saying that a reference to change enables us to make four rather than five claims for the characteristics of potentiality.

IVd. Arguments for specificity of potentialities; 1] *They are specific rather than completely indeterminate;* 2] *Potentialities are indeterminate within a specific range in three types of cases:* (a) *Contrary applications of rational capacities;* (b) *Active and imaginary applications of rational capacities;* (c) *Applications of all capacities within a quantitative or qualitative range.*

The next problem before us is to justify the assertion that there are as many as four of these claims to be made. There has to be a proof that potentialities are specific, and, subsequently, an accounting for the fact that potentialities are properties of minds and objects.

A simple example helps to prove that powers are specific. Litmus paper suffers a change in color when it is dropped into an acidic or basic solution. The crucial assumption with which we begin is that this change, like every other, is a specific kind of change; litmus turns a specific shade of pink in an acidic solution. Our object is to determine whether the potentialities which condition the occurrence of specific kinds of changes are themselves specific or indeterminate. A specific potentiality would narrowly limit the kind of change which a substance having the potentiality could produce, whereas indeterminacy might be conceived as an openness or receptivity to any kind of change.

Let us suppose that potentialities are indeterminate in order to see what this entails. A piece of litmus paper suffers a change, though on the hypothesis the paper was completely passive when the character of the change was determined. It had the potentiality for changing, but this was an indeterminate potentiality which would have made it possible for litmus to have suffered any imaginable kind of change. The assumption that powers are indeterminate evidently puts the burden for deciding the precise character of the change upon the active causal agency; in our example, this means that the acid, alone must have been responsible for the fact that the litmus turned pink. But this is no more satisfactory, because the acid is also supposed to have had an indeterminate potentiality, and, therefore, it could have modified the litmus paper in every way conceivable. Our problem then is to account for the fact that litmus has in fact turned a specific shade of pink. We have two causal conditions which have jointly produced a change in one of them, but neither of the two is fit to determine the character of the change. Under the circumstances, the causal conditions should not have been sufficient to produce the change, and it should not have occurred. Remembering that it has occurred, we have to modify our assumption.

Potentialities cannot all be indeterminate; at least one of the causal agencies must have a specific potentiality. There appears to be no logical reason for attributing this specificity to the power of the active rather than the passive causal condition, but we shall arbitrarily assume that it is the power of the acidic solution which is specific. Unhappily, this revised assumption is no better than the original one. The image we have in this case is that of a sculptor imposing form upon a rough-hewn block of marble; he chisels, and it takes on shape. We forget, however, that of marble and litmus paper each has a limited tolerance, and that form cannot be imposed upon either of them beyond a certain range of possible modifications. This is easily demonstrated by substituting glass for the marble, and newspaper for the litmus. The glass will not chip as marble does, and the newspaper may dissolve, but it will not turn pink. Arguing from the changes produced to the conditioning potentialities, we must say that litmus and marble have different specific potentialities from newspaper and glass. More generally, we may suppose that minds and objects have specific potentialities for each of the kinds of change they initiate or undergo.

The emphasis in this statement must be on the phrase "kinds of change," because it saves us from making a claim that would be too sweeping. Potentialities are no doubt specific, but this does not mean that they are in no way indeterminate. The fact that litmus can turn various shades of pink suggests that the specificity of potentialities is tempered by a measure of indeterminacy. We might speak of this as indeterminacy within specificity. Consequently, when we say that different changes justify the inference that causal conditions which produced them have different specific potentialities, we must henceforward be careful to ascertain that these changes belong to different ranges of possible effects.

There are three classes of instances in which different changes are conditioned by the same potentialities, and where the relevant potentialities are indeterminate within a range of specificity. These are: changes which result from contrary applications of a rational formula; instances where a rational formula determines the course of either action or conception; and changes which vary within a certain quantitative or qualitative range. Potentialities which condition the first two sorts of change are obviously mental capacities, but the last set of cases appears to cover the field of all changes, and it therefore concerns all potentialities.

An example of a potentiality which enables a man to act in either of two contrary ways is a doctor's skill. Having learned a certain technique, the doctor can use it to save a patient or destroy him. This is the indeterminacy of the potentiality, but its limits are just as pronounced. Surgical skill is no help to a doctor brewing tea, and it would scarcely help him to cure an infection. This is roughly Aristotle's example, and he makes the same point:

> All arts, i.e., all productive forms of knowledge, are potencies; they are originative sources of change in another thing or in the artist himself considered as other. And each of those which are accompanied by a rational formula is alike capable of contrary effects, but one nonrational power produces one effect; e.g., the hot is

capable only of heating, but the medical art can produce both disease and health. The reason is that science is a rational formula and the scientific men produce both the contrary effects.[10]

The second characteristic indeterminacy of mental dispositions reveals itself in the fact that someone with an appropriate ability can imagine how to do something or he can actually do it. Cases of this sort are different from the ones in which we imagine ourselves performing as we are incapable of doing. Consider the doctor who plans an operation before he makes the incision. This is a case in which the same potentiality, or skill, is required as a condition for either activity. It may be argued to the contrary that operations are sometimes planned by doctors with clumsy hands in order that surgeons may perform them, but this is a special instance of the cases which have already been put aside. We are concerned with a surgeon who anticipates the steps of the operation and then performs it. The same ability will condition both of these activities, though it will be supported in the latter case by certain motor skills which have nothing to do with intellectual preparation. I have so far been stressing the indeterminacy of the doctor's skill, but of course this ability is strictly determinate relative to the set of all possible actions which a man might conceivably perform: the doctor's skill enables him to respond to a very particular range of circumstances.

Turning now to the third class of cases in which potentialities are indeterminate within a range, we notice that a doctor is able to apply the same skill with varying consequences. Thus, plastic surgeons tilt noses to their customers' specifications. This is an illustration of the general point that the same potentiality may be a condition for changes which vary within a certain quantitative or qualitative range. Other examples lend support to this conclusion. Consider the athlete who runs a mile in less than four minutes. He is as capable of running a three-minute mile or a ninety-second one if the track is located on an asteroid; the smaller the planet, the less the gravitational force, and the faster he should be able to move. The relevant ability in this case is specific, but there is indeterminacy within its specificity. These first two examples have been instances of variation within a *quantitative* range. For an example of variation within a qualitative range, we return to the litmus paper. It turns more or less pink and more or less blue; and similarly, solutions which affect it have capacities for turning litmus pink or blue, but not some particular shade of either color, and so two pieces of litmus may not turn the same color in the same acid solution if one of them has been used repeatedly before.

I regard all of these examples as evidence that potentialities are indeterminate within a range, and yet, someone might object that no one of the examples is an exception to the rule that every potentiality is absolutely specific. His reason would be that we argue from changes which occur to their conditioning potentialities; and he would claim that having no other method for determining the characteristics of potentiality, we have no choice but to say that different changes entail different potentialities. The critic might add that the notion of indeterminacy within specificity presupposes some other, but in fact nonexistent method for proving that the very same potentiality conditions the occurrence of different changes.

For the purposes of evaluating this suggestion, I want to distinguish rational from nonrational capacities, in order to discuss the rational ones first. The decisive question is whether or not we have a method for proving that the potentialities which condition different changes are in fact a single potentiality, and, as it happens, we do have a method. Our normal procedure is to argue from the occurrence of different changes to the possession of different conditioning potentialities. However, when it is impossible for a man to produce either of two or a variety of changes without being able to produce the one or numerous others, we infer that the diverse changes are conditioned by a single potentiality which is indeterminate within a range. This is the principle which justifies the claim that rational capacities are indeterminate in the manner described in each of the three classes of cases mentioned above. The doctor who cannot purposely misapply a treatment cannot use it to cure; if he is unable to imagine how bones ought to be set, he is unable to set them; and last, a doctor who cannot repair arm fractures located three inches down from the elbow cannot do any better if the break occurs an inch closer to the wrist. These capacities are not separable from one another; nonpossession of one capacity within a range entails nonpossession of the remaining one or others. This is very different from the case of litmus paper, where we could easily prepare a slip of paper which becomes blue in basic solutions, but not pink in acids.

Turning at this point to the nonrational capacities, we find that the notion of absolute specificity is no more successful in accounting for them. The claim that I have been making is that these potentialities are indeterminate within a quantitative and qualitative range, and the counter-suggestion is that every change produced within such a range is conditioned by a different, specific potentiality. To answer this criticism, it will help to distinguish continuous from discrete changes, and to consider the two separately.

Suppose that we take organic growth as our example of continuous change, and concentrate upon the range of development between the point at which a plant achieves its mature form and the point at which it is full-grown. This is a unitary range in which the plant undergoes no radical qualitative change. Remembering now that our basic procedure is to argue from the fact of different changes to different, conditioning potentialities, we note that the problem is to determine how many changes occur within this range, and, thereby, how many potentialities condition the development of the plant within this span. Someone who argues that potentialities are absolutely specific will insist that there are a multiplicity of changes here, for the reason that there are an infinite number of potentialities paired off against this infinite succession of changes.

But surely this is unacceptable, for it neglects to distinguish the continuous character of change from the intellectualized notion of discrete points which we project upon that process, and, consequently, it falsifies the nature of change. In itself, change is continuous, and we err in supposing that any stage in the process is a separate change. Thus, given one, continuous change, we infer to a single, conditioning potentiality, and not to a multiplicity of them. This is typical of all continuous changes within a quantitative or qualitative range, and of changes that are suffered, as well as those that are initiated.

This raises an awkward point, because someone believing that litmus changes color within a continuous range between blue and deep pink might suggest that litmus has a single either-or potentiality rather than one power for turning pink, and one for turning blue. The power of litmus would remain specific, but the range of indeterminacy would be substantially increased. Moreover, every case where change passes through or between extreme qualitative differences would appear to justify a similar conclusion, and the specificity of potentialities would be very much compromised.

The only plausible rejoinder to this, it would seem to me, is that there are discontinuities as well as continuities in change, and that sharp qualitative differences mark the gaps. The awkwardness here is due to the practical difficulty of locating the discontinuities, but even this is not insuperable, for we discover these breaks in continuity in places such as that at which litmus, in a neutral solution, fails to turn either pink or blue. Given these discontinuous ranges of change, we can infer that there are separate potentialities conditioning their occurrence.

After continuous change, we have to consider discrete changes such as separate, shattering glasses and crumpling fenders. The man who argues for absolute specificity will claim that glasses which shatter into different numbers of pieces must have had different potentialities, but we can answer him by appealing to the criterion of non-separability. Application of this principle is slightly more difficult in the present case than it was before, because we are now considering the changes suffered by separate individuals, whereas before the changes were all caused by one man applying a rational formula. In order to overcome this difficulty, we begin by referring to the set of glasses of some kind, and we point out that no glass of this type could break into fifteen pieces if some other one could not break into twelve. Indeed, being glasses of the same kind, there is every reason to suppose that both glasses could shatter into either number of fragments. This is to say that their potentialities are indeterminate within a range.

If we suppose, as I think is true, that potentialities are not absolutely specific, we have still to account for the fact that minds and objects produce certain changes rather than others within the range of effects which these powers qualify them to produce. This is to ask why litmus turns some one shade of pink rather than another in an acid solution. The obvious explanation is that differences in the effects produced are the consequence of differences in the set of causal conditions which produce them. Litmus turns more or less pink, because the solution is more or less acidic. But having said this, I am obliged to counter suspicions that this explanation contradicts the earlier claim that changes would not occur if potentialities were indeterminate.

When the question of indeterminate potentialities was first considered, litmus and the acid solution were supposed to have potentialities which were so indeterminate as to condition the occurrence of *any* change. Under those conditions, the causal agencies would not be sufficient to determine the character of the change, and it would not occur. Our present notion of indeterminacy is not the same as that first one, however, and it does not have the unacceptable entailments of that first view. Potentialities which are indeterminate within a range do not qualify minds and objects to be causal conditions for the production of any change; substances having these powers are only qualified to produce effects within certain limits. Thus, basic solutions have only to determine what shade of blue the litmus will turn; there is no question of their forcing it to sing middle C. Under these modified circumstances, there appears to be nothing incapacitating about the notion that potentialities are indeterminate within a range of specificity. We can give an exhaustive account of why variations are produced in a range of effects by referring to substitutions which have been made in the set of causal conditions. Assembly of the causal conditions is like the preparation for staging a play. Everyone memorizes his lines and has a general idea of the character he is to do, but the action takes its precise form only as the scenes are rehearsed, and the members of the cast adjust themselves one to another. The causal conditions are different only for making no adjustment and requiring no rehearsal.

This concludes our discussion of specificity.

IVe. Possession of potentialities by minds and objects; 1] Aristotle: potentialities constitute essences of things; 2] Our problem: to find a ground for essence in actuality; 3] Solution: (a) We should concentrate on physical objects first, then generalize to cover minds; (b) Dynamic and static properties; (c) .Three arguments to show that the ground sought for potentiality is provided by properties constituting actuality of substances.

The analysis up to this point has concentrated upon potentiality's relation to the actuality which is prior to it in knowledge. There have been two reasons for this emphasis: First, reference to the effects which are produced by minds and objects is the key to inferences about the nature and function of potentialities; and, second, it is the function of powers to condition the occurrence of change, and we have required an analysis of the specificity which enables potentialities to function as conditions for change. Now however, when nothing remains to be said about function or of the characteristic specificity which enables powers to function as they do, our attention shifts from the actuality which is prior to potentiality in knowledge to the actuality which is prior in being.

This is the actuality of minds and objects having powers, and our new problem is to determine how these substances come to possess their potentialities. Function, of course, will still be implicit in our discussion to the extent that the suggested solution to our present problem will depend upon inferences which accept change as their point of reference and presuppose that powers function as logical conditions for the occurrence of change.

There is a remark in Aristotle's *Physics* which penetrates to the very heart of the issue that concerns us. Surveying the several kinds of change, Aristotle writes:

> And above all there is the case of a thing which is in motion neither accidentally nor in respect of something else belonging to it, but in virtue of being itself directly in motion. Here we have a thing which is *essentially* moveable; and that which is so is a different thing according to the particular variety of motion.[11]

The last sentence of this passage tells us that substances are distinguished from one another by virtue of the changes which they suffer and effect; and, moreover, it affirms that the variety of these changes is symptomatic of differences in essence. In order to understand this better, we have to recall that substances qualify to produce changes, because of their potentialities. As I understand him, Aristotle refers to the different effects which things produce in order to direct our attention to the potentialities which condition the occurrence of these changes. The point of his remark is that things differ essentially insofar as they possess different potentialities. This is the notion that minds and objects are to be conceived, primarily, as dynamic agencies.

The claim that things have essences is frequently disparaged, but, for the most part, these criticisms are intended for a theory which is different from the one which I have just outlined. The other conception is that science must afford us essential definitions, according to genus and specific difference, of natural substances. This program is criticized for attempting to provide a metaphysical basis for a classificatory system; critics say that the classification will be as much an expression of whim or practical interest as it is a description of natural order. As discussion will show, criticisms of this kind have no bearing upon the conception of essence which I am about to explicate. This notion is logically prior to every attempted classification of substances, because it is a partial analysis of the nature of substance.

As it stands, our conception of essence is not yet complete. Indeed, it cannot be, because as the notion is presently understood, things whose essences are their potentialities will be identified by reference to what they will eventually be or do, and there will be no recognition of what they presently are. This is unsatisfactory, because children, for example, will be known exclusively as prospective parents. Essence cannot be *wholly* constituted of specific potentialities. There must be a grounding for it in actuality. This is the transformation of our original problem; we began by asking how minds and objects can have potentialities, but for "substances-with-powers," we now read "essence," and our goal is to determine how actuality functions as a constituent of essence.

The intuitively obvious solution to this problem has already been mentioned several times. There are properties which constitute minds and objects as actualities, and for want of any other factor contributing to their actuality,[12] these properties must be the basis in actuality which is required for essence. The matter to be clarified is the relation between these properties and powers, but here again, the solution is obvious, for almost no one doubts that knives have potentialities to cut, *because* their blades have fine edges. If common sense were our arbiter, it would only remain to draw out the implications of these ideas before bringing discussion to a close. We are only prevented from doing this by the fact that orthodox reductionist Humeans have no sympathy for these common sense distinctions. The fact that knives cut is as familiar to them as to us, but they deny that knives have potentialities for cutting, and philosophically, at least, they would not be at all surprised if knives with very sharp blades ceased to be of use in slicing ordinary loaves of bread. These philosophers deny that there is an intimate connection between the form that something has and the function which it serves. It is because of their views that we are required to support our intuitive convictions with a *priori* proofs.

In formulating these arguments, I want to concentrate upon the analysis of physical objects, for the reason that properties which constitute them as actuals are more evident to us than the nonintrospectable states of minds. We can generalize our final arguments to include minds, once we are satisfied that the issues are satisfactorily resolved in the case of physical objects.

As a preliminary to the analysis, I want to introduce labels for the two sorts of properties whose relation is in question. We will talk of "static" and "dynamic" properties. Dynamic properties are specific potentialities, and, as I have been arguing, they are the properties which qualify substances for entry into causal relationships. Describing them as "dynamic" is *not* intended to imply that the potentialities are themselves in motion, or that they are *causal* conditions for motion; both of these notions have already been disclaimed. Static properties are those which constitute the actual state or condition of an object; they are its qualitative, quantitative and structural characteristics. When the object performs as a member of a set of causal conditions, it is by way of one or more of its static properties that the object suffers or initiates a change. Readers will notice a disparity between the common use of "static" and the meaning that I am giving to the term. Normally, "static" is defined as "that which is not in motion," and yet, this conflicts with my assertion that objects cause effects by way of their static properties. I have chosen to use this term, because there are no alternative adjectives for the noun, "state," and because the adjectives, "conditional" and "conditioned" are too remote from "condition" when it is used as a synonym of "state." Despite these several ambiguities, the use of these terms should facilitate discussion.

The coming argument has three parts. I wish to prove, first, that there is a necessary relation between static properties and the effects produced by objects having these properties; second, that there is also a necessary relation between the occurrence of these effects and the powers which enable objects to produce them; and last, that where static and dynamic properties are, respectively, causal and logical conditions for production of the same change, we can establish that they have a special relation to one another.

As we consider the relation between static properties and change, we notice a correlation between the effects which objects cause, and the kinds of static properties they have. I mean, for example, that black, sooty carbon-derivatives normally burn. There are countless numbers of these constant conjunctions, and though some of them may be accidental, it is evident that not all of them can be, if we assume the contrary and work out its entailments. The supposition will be that the invariant coupling of a particular change with an object having certain static properties is accidental in every case. But now recall that static properties constitute the actuality of substances, and, that substances act as causal conditions by way of their static properties. Our supposition is just the claim that the relation between an effect and its causal conditions is always accidental. Previous discussion entitles us to say that this view is mistaken; particular effects do not occur unless causes of certain kinds produce them.

Our second problem is to determine what relation holds between these effects and specific potentialities; but like the one before, this question has already been settled. We have said that possession of a power is a logically necessary condition for the production of a change. This is the point of convergence which we have anticipated. In order to produce a certain effect, substances must have specific potentialities which logically condition the occurrence, and appropriate static properties. The difficulty here is to tell how these two sorts of properties are related, and the solution, I believe, is to say that objects have some specific potentialities rather than others, because they have static properties of certain kinds.

IVe. 4] *Two* arguments proving *that the being and char-acter of potentialities are contingent upon the char-acter of properties which determine how things shall exist as actuals;* 5] *Generalization of this principle to cover minds; minds are constituted as actuals of nonintrospectable mental states;* F. *Further char-acteristics of potentiality now determinable;* 1] *Modification of potentialities;* 2] *Endurance of potentialities;* G. *A popular misconception about real potentiality.*

Admittedly, this is only one of the two possible conclusions which can be inferred from the claims which have been made about static and dynamic properties. It is at least conceivable that an object's static properties do not determine what its powers are even though both sorts of properties are required if it is to contribute to the production of a change. Nonetheless, a simple conceptual experiment proves that our solution is the only acceptable one.

Imagine a lump of coal which is a mixture of nothing but carbon and a number of metallic elements. If we extract the carbon, the coal will be unable to burn, and there will be a measure of plausibility to the counter-suggestion which I have just mentioned. It might now be the case that only one of the conditions for burning coal, the static properties of carbon, has been removed. The potentiality for burning might be a wholly separate condition, and it might still be present in the coal-minus-carbon. In order to show the absurdity of this claim, we have to put the carbon back into the coal, and systematically purify the conglomerate of each of the other elements composing it. Notice that the extraction of each of these makes no difference to the coal's potentiality for burning. Ultimately, we are left with pure carbon, and at this point, coal as an actual is constituted by the static properties which go under the name "carbon." Supposing, as is true, that the coal still has the potentiality for burning, we can only account for its possession of the property by referring to these characteristic static properties of carbon. Our conclusion is that the static properties which identify carbon are both necessary and sufficient for its having the capacity to burn.

Perhaps the response will be that this single instance is not an adequate proof of the claim that the being and character of a thing's potentialities are contingent upon its static properties, and so, in order to put the matter beyond doubt, I suggest one last variation on a familiar *reductio*. Let us suppose that objects have static properties and dynamic properties, but that the fact of having certain static properties is not sufficient to determine that the object should also have certain dispositions. But if this is the case, what would determine the identity of a thing's dispositions? What is left to determine them? It seems to me that nothing remains to decide the issue, unless we assume that the world is presided over by a demon who rules on matters of this sort. But if we deny his existence, or merely that he interferes, and if we also suppose that static properties have no part in fixing the identity of a thing's powers, then it will follow that nothing determines their identity. In these circumstances, we should expect that different lumps of coal would have different potentialities. Some of them might burn, but others might sprout roots and grow into tulip trees. Anything might happen when a set of causal conditions was assembled, and it would be impossible to predict what a thing's likely behavior would be if we had never seen it perform in the past. We could expect the disordered universe which is entailed by suppositions like this one. For the failure of experience to display itself in this way, we have to deny the premise. Our general conclusion is that substances have powers because of their static properties, and moreover, that they have some powers rather than others, because of the identity of their static properties.[13]

Having located the actuality which grounds potentiality in physical objects, we are now free to generalize the account so as to include the capacities of minds. Their analysis was originally delayed, for the reason that nonintrospectable mental states, the mental counterparts of properties like mass and micro-structure in physical objects, cannot be described as observables (unless we adopt the mind-body identity thesis). This consideration would have made it awkward to have used these states as examples in the arguments which I have now proposed. Nonetheless, it was established in the chapter preceding this one that mental states endure, and that they constitute the actuality of minds in the same way that properties like mass constitute the actuality of physical objects. Given this assumption, one of its nonintrospectable states will be to mind as the edge of its blade is to a knife, and, carrying over the principle which has just been demonstrated, we can say that minds have the capacities they do, because of being constituted of some nonintrospectable states rather than others. When powers are in question, the analysis of mind is nearly parallel to the analysis of physical objects; and this claim is independent of assumptions about the identity of minds and bodies.

This completes our discussion of the substantive matters in question, and it presents an opportunity for taking our bearings. The major issue has been to determine how actuals come to have potentialities, and, as restated, this has become the problem of finding a ground in actuality for powers. The solution has been that things have the potentialities they do, because of the character of their mental states and static properties. This is to say that substances differ essentially, because they have different mental states or static properties, and, consequently, different potentialities.

Readers who are inclined to be suspicious of any realist theory of powers may well believe that the theory which I have proposed is no challenge to their own views since, as it will appear to them, I have now abandoned the claim that potentialities are real. As a man of their persuasion might ask: What reason have we to deny that potentiality is reducible to actuality, when it is not merely admitted, but argued that the character and the very being of potentialities is dependent upon properties which constitute substances as actuals? Isn't this tantamount to saying that potentiality is not a distinct mode of being, and that everything real is actual?

I think the reasons for denying the reducibility of potentiality are the several arguments which have either proved or reinforced the claim that there is a categorical distinction between actuality and potentiality. More recent arguments have not compromised this distinction. Their only consequence has been to validate the claim that actuality is prior to potentiality in being. Having previously concentrated upon the irreducible differences in essence, we have now demonstrated the interdependence of its parts, and, thereby, its unity.

The fact of this unity helps us to clarify an ambiguity which I have previously been unable to eliminate. It was argued in Chapter 1 that mind owes its potentialities to its mental states, and that these powers qualify the mind to act as a causal condition. In order to minimize confusion, I neglected to add that mind acts as a causal condition by way of these mental states, though as a substitute I claimed that mind acts as a causal condition because it has a power to be one. The reason for this possibly misguided subtlety was my concern that a complete statement of the position would be rejected as paradoxical. The argument would have been that the mind having a certain mental state cannot be a causal condition, unless a certain power has been acquired, but that having the power is dependent upon having the mental state. The critical reply would have been that we have no use for the potentiality; a mind having the required mental state would have seemed qualified to enter a causal relationshp, and to be a causal condition. The error in this response has subsequently been exposed by distinguishing dynamic and static properties, while insisting upon their relatedness.

There is something about the mutuality of this relationship which remains disconcerting, but this is a consequence of the method we use in doing metaphysical analyses. A completed analysis is usually sequential in form, as we describe the logically most prior elements of the matter in question, before going on to those which are less fundamental. Frequently, however, there are various perspectives from which to describe this subject matter, and when that happens, the elements will have different relative priorities as the perspective changes.

This is the reason, I think, that we suspect an intolerable circularity in the theory which I have outlined. It requires that we argue from three different standpoints, and in each case, the features of essence display themselves to us in a different logical order. Analyzing substances as causal conditions, we emphasize their static properties, because effects are suffered and initiated by way of these properties. From another angle, the effects produced are the clue that substances must have powers which qualify them to be causal conditions. And from a third standpoint, we account for the fact that substances have these powers by referring once again to the properties which constitute things as actuals. We dispel the illusion of paradox by reminding ourselves that these shifts in direction and logical priority are all on the side of the intellectual analysis, and that the unity of actuality and potentiality in essence is the underlying theme, and the object of inquiry.

I wish to emphasize one last advantage of the Aristotelian conception of essence. This is the fact that it enables us to describe several more characteristics of dispositional properties, and thereby to resolve certain traditional problems in their analysis. One characteristic is that dispositions are acquired and changed. In order to explain this, we have only to remember that the possession of potentialities is dependent upon a thing's static properties or mental states. This justifies us in saying that dispositions are acquired or changed as mental states and static properties are modified in some way. It is also the explanation for that puzzling claim that there are potentialities for acquiring potentialities. As an example of this, we have the man who has a facility for languages, which he studies and learns to speak. We account for this by saying that the man has a nonintrospectable mental state which is susceptible to modification. When this change is produced, there will also be an alteration in the mind's capacities, as the capacity for suffering this change to the mental state is replaced by the ability to use a language.

And finally, we are in a position to demonstrate that potentialities endure. This follows from two points which have been made. First, potentialities are not dependent for their being upon the establishment of a causal relationship, because causal relationships would never arise, if substances did not already have the powers to be causal conditions. This is just half of the argument we require, for it shows that potentiality is logically prior to the production of effects, but it does not establish that powers endure when changes are not being produced. There is still the possibility that substances come to have powers at the moment before the last supplementary condition is fulfilled, and the effect is produced. But this is occasionalism, and we are free to reject it, because the notion that powers condition change has been supplemented by the claim that the being and character of potentialities is dependent upon the static properties and mental states which constitute the actuality of substances. Properties like mass endure through the intervals when bodies are not producing effects, and consequently we may say that the powers of these substances also endure. This proves that Austin was perfectly right when he criticized the "shall-if" analysis of "can" statements for entailing the contrary.

Endurance and susceptibility to change are the last two characteristics of the six which have now been credited to potentiality. Being a condition for the production of change, being irreducible to actuality, and being specific while depending upon actuality for this specificity are the other four. I admit that this enumeration is no adequate substitute for a definition of potentiality, but remembering that there cannot be a definition, I think we shall have to accept this, or some other fragmentary list, as a substitute for a neat formula telling us exactly what potentiality is.

One last comment is in order. Surveying our list, we find no mention of a realm of would-be happenings which are claimed to be shadow images of past or prospective events in the world. This, of course, is the interpretation which empiricists give to all realist accounts of potentiality before they remind us that theories of this kind have no place in rigorous philosophic thought. Happily, there is general agreement about this; hardly any realist, and certainly not Aristotle, has ever supported such a view. When realists say that a statue exists potentially, they mean, I suggest, that there exist substances having the powers to produce it. There is a would-be statue only as there is a piece of bronze, and a man who can wield a hammer in a way that will reshape the bronze. Empiricists forget that the arguments which prove the irreducibility of potentiality to actuality are rules which oblige us not to conceive of potentialities as though they were pseudo-actualities.

Some recapitulation is expected of us. Our discussion began with an analysis of Hume's theory that abstract ideas are determinate images bound to a power. We decided that Hume admits the reality of powers in order to account for the fact that minds can think of series of ideas when action or an intellectual need prompts them to do so. This preliminary discussion focused our attention upon the relation between causality and powers, because Hume was interpreted as arguing that powers qualify minds to conceive of relevant ideas when they are acted upon by causal conditions. Subsequent analysis explored the characteristics of this relation, and of causality and powers themselves. It was said that causes and effects are related by way of production and existential dependence, and that powers are the real potentialities which qualify minds and objects to produce effects. Finally, we were led to give a more detailed account of potentialities, and we concluded that they depend for their being and character upon the properties which constitute the actuality of substances.

This conception of powers is likely to be criticized for being incomplete or misconceived, and I want to end the discussion by defending myself against these objections.

There is a passage in Aristotle which might seem to confirm the belief that I have given only a partial analysis of dispositions. Aristotle lists the following meanings of "potency":

> 1] a source of movement or change, which is in another thing then the thing moved or in the same thing qua other . . . 2] the source of a thing's being moved by another thing or by itself qua other . . . 3] the capacity of performing this well or according to intention . . . So too 4] in the case of passivity. — 5] The state in virtue of which things are absolutely impassive or unchangeable.[1]

The fifth meaning of the term is evidently in conflict with the other four. It refers to powers which enable substances to resist change, while they describe the powers which condition change.

There are two things to be said about this discrepant fifth sense of the word. First, potencies for resisting change are not on a par with the potentialities which condition change. As Aristotle, himself, writes: ". . . the proper definition of the primary kind of potency will be 'a source of change in another thing or in the same thing qua other.' "[2] Potentiality in this primary sense is the only power to which we must refer in accounting for either the occurrence or the non-occurrence of change. As an example, consider a product advertised as "rust proof." Rather than saying that it has a potency for resisting change, we merely infer that it has no potentiality for rusting. Second, the fifth meaning of "potency" is native to a kind of higher-level talk about the potentialities which condition change. We say that a mind or object resists change in particular circumstances, but this is no more than an elliptical way of pointing out that it does not have the capacity for helping to produce a certain change.

Next, I want to take up four reputed misconceptions which are often charged against realist theories of dispositions. First, there is the traditional claim that the realist conception only plays upon the analyticity of certain statements. Realists insist that things have powers to act as they do, but, so the objection goes, there is nothing informative about the claim that things can act as they are already acting. I think that the foregoing arguments have established that there is something informative about this notion; but moreover, the analyticity of statements like "Opium induces sleep because of having a dormitive power" is merely the evidence that we have adopted a simple convention. We have agreed that the term used to characterize a disposition should be the one that is used to describe the change which is conditioned by it. But surely this rule is commonsensical enough; what more appropriate term could we use for referring to a power? This trivial analyticity deserves none of the attention which reductionists normally give to it.

A second possible objection to the realist theory has to do with a matter of interpretation. It might be said that I have proposed a doctrine of internal relations, even though I reject this understanding of the claim that dispositional properties are real potentialities. The reason for contention here is that the best-known theory of internal relations is the absolute idealist one which holds that a complete understanding of the relatedness of substances in the world would reveal that the identity of each substance is determined by its relations to every other one. This theory is in general disrepute, and anyone who equates the realist theory of powers with this view is likely to suppose that he has a more than adequate excuse for denying that powers are real potentialities. He is mistaken, however, because there is no similarity between the idea of real potentiality and the idealist theory. The realist doctrine holds that a thing's potentialities limit the changes for which it can be responsible, and to this extent, the doctrine is atomistic in its implications. There is nothing here to support the claim that all substances are related in the mind of God.

Let me add that the idea of real potentiality is not any sort of claim about internal relations. Causal relations are the only ones which are of interest to the realist theory, and far from being internal, it supposes that they are as empirically obvious as the cause of wet boots during a walk on a rainy day. All that is internal, meaning what is inferred and cannot be perceived, are the dispositional properties.

The third objection to be considered would have us believe that essentialist doctrines like mine are of no use to science. It reminds us that scientists are concerned with the observable faces of things, and that they have nothing to learn from inferences which account for observable activity by referring to occult properties. And consequently, because the conceptual needs of science are supposed to be our standard of what is significant in philosophy, a realist theory of powers is valueless. Putting aside the very dubious appeal to this standard of what is philosophically relevant, the issue wanting clarification is the assumption that scientists have no use for the idea of real potentialities. If this means that realist theories never enter scientific consciousness, there is nothing disastrous for us in that. More to the point is the question of whether scientists would have an object for study if powers were not real. If my arguments have any validity, the answer to this question is that a world without powers would be chaotic, unamenable to scientific description. Furthermore, scientists tacitly acknowledge the reality of powers in their descriptions of nature. This is evident in their assumption that causal-law statements cover the behavior of all of the members of a class of objects even though very few of these objects have been tested. As I understand it, this is recognition that all of the members of the class have the powers to act as causal-law statements hold that they would act if they were tested. Under the circumstances, it is precipitate to deny that the claims of realist metaphysics have no value for science. It seems more correct to say that realists articulate and justify the assumptions which scientists make, but never defend.

There are other possible objections to the theory which I have tried to revive, but one of them in particular raises the fundamental issue in dispute. My problem has been to discover why it happens that different substances produce different effects, and my answer has been, first, that these substances are things of different kinds, and, second, that the phrase "different kinds" refers to the properties which constitute the actuality of substances and also to the real potentialities which qualify substances to act as causal agencies. The response to this may well be that these are mere slogans, and that my analysis is interesting only as a symptom of that rational impulse to continue giving explanations long past the time when there is anything to be explained. Say that observable fact shows a correlation between variations in sets of causal conditions and variations in their effects, but make no pretense that you explain these constant conjunctions by talking about the "efficacy" of kinds or by elaborating upon the misleading implications of expressions such as "potentiality"; remember that you began by calling our attention to the fact that changes occur in the world, and admit that your arguments have never carried us beyond that starting point. So far as your remarks are not tautologies or stipulative definitions, there is no cognitive value to any one of them which is not translatable into an assertion describing matters of fact.

In effect, this is an *a priori* criticism of all attempts to establish the reality of categorical factors like causal laws, powers and moral principles. It supposes that all our ideas of the world must be ostensively definable, and, thereby eliminating reason, it assures that thought will be incapable of transcending the immediately given. The motive for this attack is a desire to control excessive metaphysical speculation. Given the notorious variety of metaphysical theories, empiricists find it easier to say that all of these theories are meaningless than to adjudicate among them. Very little is said, however, about the fact that this most extravagant of all philosophical notions washes out not only all of metaphysics, but all of science as well. No general statement will be meaningful if the empiricists are correct, and, remembering that even "red" is a general term, we discover that their conception of meaning and truth would have us all acting like Cratylus, who restricted himself to waggling a finger at the passing flux.

The alternative to skepticism is to agree that we do have ideas of reason, and to admit that we can use these ideas for making claims about the world. We already do both of these things when we say that there are causal laws while knowing full well that the laws are not reducible to any set of observables. Another example is our belief that physical objects are sources of our perceptions, and that they cannot be equated with any set of observations. Both of these are examples of metaphysical ideas, but we adopt them, because consciously or not, we believe that experience would be radically different from what it is, if nature were deprived of its causal laws and physical objects.

This suggests a principle which is intermediate between verifiability and a *carte blanche* invitation to metaphysical theorizing. We say that no metaphysical idea is acceptable, unless the reality of the factor in question must be presupposed in order to account for some categorical feature of experience. This is the principle which I have tried to satisfy in analyzing the notion of dispositional properties. The observable fact that causes produce effects has provided a control upon the inferences that were drawn, and arguments have then established, it seems to me, that the reality of powers is a necessary condition for the production of these effects.

Introduction

1. Austin, John, "Ifs and Cans," *Philosophical Papers*, eds. J. Urmson and G. Warnock (London: Oxford University Press, 1961), pp. 153–80.

2. *Ibid.*, pp. 162–63.

3. *Ibid.*, p. 163.

4. For want of another expression, I am forced to use "state" in two ways. The first sense is a generic one covering various properties including dispositions, and referring to the on-going condition of a substance. In its other sense, "state" will be used in the expressions "mental states" and "static properties." These will be used to refer to properties which differ categorically from dispositional properties, as actuality differs from potentiality.

5. Nowell-Smith, Philip, *Ethics* (Harmondsworth: Penguin Books, 1954), p. 278.

6. *Ibid.*, p. 278.

7. Austin, "Ifs and Cans," p. 176.

8. I, like Austin, am supposing the "shall-if" analysis of "can" sentences to be one equating the having of a disposition with satisfaction of *both* of two conditions; these are, the testing of the object to which a dispositional predicate is to be assigned, and the fact of its responding in a certain way. With Austin, I am *not* supposing that the "shall-if" analysis should be interpreted as a case of material implication; in that event it would be proper to ascribe a disposition even if the test conditions, referred to in the antecedent of a conditional statement, were not satisfied. There are two reasons for viewing the "shall-if" analysis as Austin has done. First, the nuance of a conditional statement used in ordinary speech

strongly inclines us to say that the statement is not true when its antecedent is false and its consequent is true. Ordinary language permits us to say that the statement may be true when neither condition is satisfied and the statement is uttered as a subjunctive conditional, but here the admission of possible truth is predicated upon the conviction that a conditional is certainly true only where there are arguments for both its antecedent and consequent. Second, we shall see in Chapter 2 that empiricists, and Carnap in particular, prescribe that both these conditions must be satisfied before it may be said that a dispositional predicate is properly introduced. Carnap seeks to eliminate dispositional predicates in favor of sentences describing test conditions and their effect, and he stipulates, in accord with the bias of ordinary linguistic usage, that both of these conditions must be satisfied if a dispositional predicate is to be introduced by way of a conditional statement.

There is one factor which very much complicates this "shall-if" analysis of dispositional predicates. This is the empiricist claim that their analysis enables us to eliminate 'can' sentences and dispositional predicates in favor of causal law statements. Law statements are normally counterfactuals describing how events must be correlated given the satisfaction of test conditions which may not now prevail. Empiricists, with few exceptions, have regarded these statements as examples of material implication, and they have said that the statements are true when their antecedents are false. Remembering that elimination of "can" sentences requires satisfaction of both the antecedent and consequent of a "shall-if" sentence, our problem in Chapter 2 will be to show how empiricists square the counterfactual character of law statements with the requirements of their analysis of "can" sentences and dispositional predicates.

9. Kant, Immanuel, *Prolegomena to any Future Metaphysics*, trans. Lewis White Beck (New York: Liberal Arts Press, 1950), p. 27. Especially, the phrase ". . . may by its own deeds be investigated and measured."

1. *Hume:*
His Realist Sympathies and Reductionist Convictions

1. Hume, David, *Treatise of Human Nature*, ed. L. A. Selby-Bigge (London: Oxford University Press, 1955), p. 17.
2. *Ibid.,* p. 18.
3. *Ibid.,* p. 18.

4. *Ibid.,* p. 20.
5. *Ibid.,* p. 24.
6. *Ibid.,* p. 24.
7. *Ibid.,* p. 18.
8. *Ibid.,* p. 261.
9. *Ibid.,* p. 423.
10. Goodman, Nelson, *Fact, Fiction and Forecast* (London: Athlone Press, 1954), pp. 17–24.
11. Hume, *Treatise of Human Nature,* p. 21.
12. Objections like this one presuppose that Hume's reductionist arguments are the standard against which everything else he wrote is to be measured. But realists would have equal justification for espousing elimination or re-interpretation of Hume's reductionist claims. Both programs are arbitrary, and we are better advised to admit that Hume has made conflicting statements in different parts of the same book. There are in fact numerous passages in which Hume makes it clear that he conceives of the association of ideas in terms of a strictly deterministic causal model. There are categorical statements to this effect on pages 135 and 165 of the *Treatise.*
13. Hume, *Treatise of Human Nature,* p. 313.
14. Hempel, C. and Oppenheim, P., "The Logic of Explanation," in *Readings in the Philosophy of Science,* eds. H. Feigl and M. Brodbeck (New York: Appleton, Century, Crofts, 1953), p. 339.
15. Hume, *Treatise of Human Nature,* p. 179.
16. *Ibid.,* p. 155.
17. *Ibid.,* p. 165.
18. *Ibid.,* p. 157.
19. *Ibid.,* p. 463.
20. *Ibid.,* p. 172.
21. *Ibid.,* p. 161.
22. *Ibid.,* p. 157.
23. *Ibid.,* p. 207.
24. Hegel, G. W. F., *Hegel's Lesser Logic, from the Encyclopaedia of the Philosophical Sciences,* trans. by W. Wallace (London: Oxford University Press, 1950), pp. 81–82.
25. Hume, *Treatise of Human Nature,* p. 69.
26. *Ibid.,* p. 172.
27. *Ibid.,* p. 173.

2. *Counterfactual Conditionals*

1. Goodman, Nelson, *Fact, Fiction and Forecast* (London: Athlone Press, 1954), p. 45.

2. Pap, Arthur, *Elements of Philosophical Analysis* (New York: The Macmillan Company, 1949), p. 213n.

3. Ryle, Gilbert, *The Concept of Mind* (London: Hutchinson and Company, 1960), p. 121.

4. Carnap, Rudolf, *The Logical Syntax of Language* (London: Routledge, and Kegan Paul, 1959), p. 321.

5. Carnap, Rudolf, "Theoretical Concepts," *Minnesota Studies in Philosophy of Science*, vol. 1, eds. H. Feigl and M. Scriven (Minneapolis: University of Minnesota Press, 1962), p. 64.

6. Carnap, Rudolf, "Testability and Meaning," *Readings in the Philosophy of Science*, eds. H. Feigl and M. Brodbeck (New York: Appleton, Century, Crofts, 1953), p. 54. For Carnap's detailed exposition of reduction sentences, pp. 53–54. Note, especially, the conditions which have to be fulfilled in order to justify the introduction of a dispositional predicate: "Here, Q_1 and Q_4 may describe experimental conditions which we have to fulfill in order to find out whether or not a certain space-time point b has the property Q_3." (p. 53); "We see that the sentences R_1 and R_2 tell us how we may determine whether or not the predicate Q_3 is to be attributed to a certain point, provided we are able to determine whether or not the four predicates Q_1, Q_2, Q_4 and Q_5 are to be attributed to it." (p. 53); "Here the pair can be replaced by one sentence . . . which means: if we accomplish the condition Q_1, then the point has the property if and only if we find the result Q_2." (p. 54); "If we establish one reduction pair (or one bilateral reduction sentence) as valid in order to introduce a predicate Q_3, the meaning of Q_3 is not established completely, but only for the cases in which the test condition is fulfilled." (p. 56) As these passages make clear, it will not do to say that the only function of reduction sentences is to provide a partial interpretation of the meaning of dispositional predicates by way of general statements describing the circumstances in which these terms might be introduced into a reconstructed scientific language without violating a logical rule or physical law. Though this may have been Carnap's original intention, his formulation of the notion of reduction sentences shows that these sentences are conceived as references to particular test conditions and their effects. They are test reports, and they introduce dispositional predicates solely on the basis of experiments performed.

7. Pap, Arthur, *Elements of Philosophical Analysis*, p. 213n.

8. Carnap, "Testability and Meaning," p. 61.

9. This interpretation is clearly acknowledged, at one point, by Carnap, himself: ". . . the (dispositional) state is not the same as (the) reactions. . . . The state of being electrically charged is not the same as the process of attracting other bodies. . . . They are consequences of the state . . . symptoms for it; but are not identical with it." "Logical Foundations of the Unity of Science," *International Encyclopedia of Unified Science* (Chicago: University of Chicago Press, 1939), vol. 1, n. 1, p. 59. Also see, Goodman, *Fact, Fiction and Forecast*, p. 60, n.11.

10. Carnap, "Theoretical Concepts," p. 63.

11. Carnap, "Testability and Meaning," pp. 59–60.

12. *Ibid.,* p. 59.

13. *Ibid.,* p. 56.

14. Braithwaite, R. B., *Scientific Explanation* (Cambridge: Cambridge University Press, 1959), pp. 301–2.

15. *Ibid.,* pp. 302–3.

16. This may appear to be too strong a criterion of nonaccidental conjunction, because it would make an accident of a succession of events which we usually do not call accidental conjuncts. We may, for example, imagine that gates close at a railroad crossing immediately after the red warning light blinks and the bell jangles. We customarily deny that it is an accident when these events occur in succession, because we know that they are all effects of the same sufficient condition, meaning, of course, the engine which has tripped a switch up the line. But despite the fact that this succession of events is not accidental in that respect, it remains accidental in the one respect in which I am interested: non-occurrence of any one of the events would have made no difference to either of the others.

17. Braithwaite, *Scientific Explanation,* p. 303.

18. Pap, *Elements of Analytic Philosophy,* pp. 206–7.

19. I suggest that the metaphysical foundations of Goodman's theory of projection are as mistaken as are those of Braithwaite's view; and for the same reason. Goodman emphasizes that some hypotheses are better grounded in past observations than others, but he fails to consider that no general statement would be likely to be better grounded than any other, if, as he supposes, there are no necessary relations in nature. Hume has said that anything could follow anything under these circumstances, and, indeed, if causal relations were as he describes them, "could" should be read as "would," because nature *would be* chaotic. No predicate would

be projectible, unless we projected "grue" using it to mean "anything or everything; or nothing at all." Goodman, *Fact, Fiction and Forecast,* Chapter Four.

3. *The Existence of Nonintrospectable Mental States*

1. Wittgenstein, Ludwig, *Philosophical Investigations,* trans. G. E. M. Anscombe (Oxford: Basil Blackwell, 1962), ¶ 5.

2. *Ibid.,* ¶ 208.

3. *Ibid.,* ¶ 208.

4. Wittgenstein, Ludwig, *The Blue and Brown Books* (Oxford: Basil Blackwell, 1958), pp. 120–21.

5. Wittgenstein, *Philosophical Investigations,* ¶ 157.

6. *Ibid.,* ¶ 156.

7. Introspectionist explanations of intelligent behavior are rejected, because, as Wittgenstein points out in paragraphs 35 and 168 of the *Investigations,* it is not necessary that intelligent conduct should always be preceded by the awareness of a peculiarly relevant introspectable phenomenon. Wittgenstein recognizes that we sometimes refer to an imagined color chart, for example, before acting, but he insists that the imagined chart is not important for its having been imagined; a real color chart would have done as well (par. 141). There is little or no realization that a sufficient condition for intelligent conduct may be as important as a necessary one: in the absence of a real color chart, someone who could not imagine the colors might be unable to act. Physiological explanations are dismissed, as in paragraph 158 of the *Investigations,* on the grounds that we know too little about the brain to suppose that references to it can serve as explanations of intelligent behavior. Wittgenstein's rejection of the mental faculty theory will be considered in detail later in the chapter.

8. Wittgenstein, *Philosophical Investigations,* ¶ 154.

9. *Ibid.,* ¶ 283.

10. *Ibid.,* ¶ 26.

11. *Ibid.,* ¶ 270.

12. *Ibid.,* ¶ 45.

13. *Ibid.,* ¶ 293.

14. Malcolm, Norman, "Wittgenstein's *Philosophical Investigations,*" *The Philosophy of Mind,* ed. Vere C. Chappell (Englewood Cliffs: Prentice-Hall, 1962), p. 93.

15. Wittgenstein, *Philosophical Investigations,* ¶ 649.

16. Wittgenstein, *The Blue and Brown Books,* pp. 120–21.

17. Wittgenstein, *Philosophical Investigations,* ¶ 157. A similar point is made in ¶ 145 where Wittgenstein asks how far a student learning a series must continue it before we have the "right" to say that he has mastered the system. Wittgenstein does not say that the statement "He has learned the system" would be meaningless if uttered when only a single correct entry had been made, but he does say that we cannot be satisfied that the student has learned to use the system if he is not regularly successful in continuing the series. I infer that we would have no right to make the assertion "He has learned the system" in these circumstances, and that, as in the case of reading, the assertion would be meaningless if made in these circumstances.

18. *Ibid.,* ¶ 157.

19. *Ibid.,* ¶ 199.

20. Wittgenstein, *The Blue and Brown Books,* p. 121.

21. For a different view, cf. Malcolm, "Wittgenstein's *Philosophical Investigations,*" p. 94.

22. Wittgenstein, *Philosophical Investigations,* ¶ 272.

23. *Ibid.,* ¶ 158.

24. Wittgenstein, *The Blue and Brown Books,* p. 120.

25. Wittgenstein, *Philosophical Investigations,* ¶ 143.

26. *Ibid.,* ¶ 163.

27. *Ibid.,* ¶ 200.

28. *Ibid.,* ¶ 146.

29. *Ibid.,* ¶ 198.

30. *Ibid.,* ¶ 201.

31. *Ibid.,* ¶ 219.

4. *Real Potentiality*

1. Aristotle, *Metaphysics,* trans. W. D. Ross, in *The Basic Works of Aristotle,* ed. by Richard McKeon (New York: Random House, 1941, 1048a31–1048b8). The sharp distinction that Aristotle draws between actuality and potentiality may raise a terminological difficulty. We often suppose that if something is not actual, it is not real. Consequently, if potentiality is not actual, it must be nothing at all, or a subsistent quasi-actuality. Aristotle has *neither* of these alternatives in mind. He supposes that both actuality and potentiality have the reality of modes of being; and that potentiality is no less real for being a different mode from actuality.

2. *Ibid.,* 1045b36–1046a3.

3. Ross, W. D., *Aristotle's Metaphysics* (London: Oxford University Press, 1924), vol. 2, p. 251.

4. Aristotle, *Metaphysics*, 1049b13.

5. *Ibid.*, 1046b29–32.

6. Aristotle, *Physics*, trans. R. P. Hardie and R. K. Gaye, in McKeon, *The Basic Works of Aristotle*, 201a10.

7. Aristotle, *Metaphysics*, 1047a10–17.

8. Ross, *Aristotle's Metaphysics*, vol. 1, p. cxxxvi.

9. Aristotle, *Metaphysics*, 1047a17–23.

10. *Ibid.*, 1046b2–20.

11. Aristotle, *Physics*, 224a27–29.

12. I am making no distinction here between form and matter, though it may well be that this distinction is ultimately required if there is to be an account of the unity of a substance amidst the diversity of its properties.

13. It should be pointed out that determination of the character of potentialities by properties constituting the actuality of substances does not entail that there is an infinite series of potentialities relating any static property to some relevant dynamic one. This, of course, is the charge likely to be made by a critic eager to show that intolerable consequences result when the if-it-does-it-can rule of inference is rigorously applied from the point of view of a realist theory of powers. Momentarily agreeing that the doing of something presupposes the having of a real potentiality, the critic will argue that a static property determining the character of a dynamic one must have a disposition for doing so. If it is then argued (by a realist such as myself) that the character of this last named disposition is also determined by the character of the static property, it will follow that there must have been a further disposition conditioning that determination, and so on. This argument strives to discredit the realist interpretation of the if-it-does-it-can rule by showing that application of the rule has the consequence that a static property *cannot* determine the character of a dynamic one; it cannot, the critic will say, for the reason that rigorous application of the rule entails that there must be a series of potentialities which though required to connect the static and dynamic property cannot connect them because of being a regress whose infinite extension precludes its completion. Arguing that the realist interpretation of this rule affords this unsatisfactory result, the critic will have us believe that we should scrap the realist interpretation and any conclusions derived by applying the rule so interpreted. Our analy-

sis of real potentiality will then be a shambles, for the whole point of our analysis has been to justify the realist interpretation of this rule. Only the critic will be satisfied now, for the analysis of dispositions will be as problematic as before, and his own account, more likely than not a reductionist one, may again seem a plausible alternative. The critic's error is to suppose that it is legitimate to apply the if-it-does-it-can rule, as realists understand it, in these circumstances. Contrary to his assumption, the realist interpretation of this principle has been validated only for application to the analysis of situations in which sets of causal conditions produce effects; it is in these cases alone that I have justified the claim that determination of the character of one factor by another presupposes that the first must possess a special capacity. I have provided no warrant for applying this rule to cases, like the present one, where the relation of static properties to dynamic ones is not that of cause and effect, but rather the relation of ground and consequent binding categorical factors which are logical constituents of substance. Acknowledging that the realist interpretation of the if-it-does-it-can rule is misapplied in this instance, we see that there are no grounds for interposing a series of dispositions between a static property and its determination of the character of a dynamic one. Possession of a certain molecular structure will determine that paper shall have the capacity to burn, but though it is conceivable that there might have been other worlds where this structure determined that paper should rust rather than burn, we have no reason to suppose that the determination is, or would be, any less than direct in either case.

Epilogue

1. Aristotle, *Metaphysics*, 1019a15–29.
2. *Ibid.*, 1020a4–6.

INDEX

Abilities: and dispositions, 16
Abstract ideas: Berkeley's theory of, 18, 19, 20; Hume's theory of, 18–28, 50–51, 76–77; and determinate ideas, 18–28 *passim*, 50, 76, 77; and represented ideas, 18–28 *passim*, 50, 51, 76, 77; and power, 19–28, 76–77; and signs, 22, 23, 24, 28, 50, 51; and causality, 26–28, 29–30, 76–77; five factors of, 30
Accidental conjunction: defined, 36, 42, 207; and causal relationship, 36–37, 43, 81, 87, 108, 111–13, 114; and spatial and temporal relationships, 42, 112, 113, 207; conditionals describing, 90, 95, 109–110, 111–13; experiments for, 95, 109–10
Actuality: and potentiality, 14, 15, 61–63, 65, 71, 119, 159, 162–63, 166, 169–71, 182–91 *passim*, 192, 209; and essence, 184, 189. *See also* Nonintrospectable mental states; Static properties
Algebraic formulae: and synthesis of recognition, 140; Wittgenstein's use of, 147–56 *passim*
Apperception: transcendental unity of, 138, 141, 144. *See also* Apprehension; Recognition; Reproduction
Apprehension: synthesis of, 138–39, 140–41, 143, 144
Aristotle: on real potentiality, 28, 71, 159, 160–62, 166–69, 171–72, 183, 193, 194–95, 209; on formal cause, 59; on causal laws, 59; on *universalia in rebus*, 59; on substance,

160–61, 167, 169, 183; on the Megarian argument, 166–69; on possibility and necessity, 168–69; on mental activity, 177–78; on essence, 183
Atoms: causal conditions and effects conceived as, 80; temporal, 139
Austin, John: analysis of "can" and "could have" sentences, 4–5, 7, 9–10, 11, 28, 55, 56, 89, 118, 192, 203

Behaviorism: and mental activity, 15, 120–22, 128–38, 147–58; Wittgenstein's 15–16, 120–37, 147–58; and the observer, 129–37 *passim*, 147–57 *passim*; and verifiability, 133, 135–36, 137, 152, 156–57
Berkeley, George: on disposition, 7; on abstract ideas, 18, 19, 20
Braithwaite, R. B.: on causal law statements, 91, 108–13

Calculus: of formalized scientific theories, 104–6
"Can" and "could have" sentences: "shall-if" and "should have-if" analysis of, 4, 9–10, 55, 89, 166, 192; and "if"-clauses, 4–5; and opportunity, 5, 10; and dispositions, 5–6, 7–8, 9–10, 55, 86, 89, 166, 192; are indicative, 5–10 *passim*; as predictions, 8, 9; as normative statements, 10; and desire, 10; and causal laws, 55; and causal law statements, 89
Capacities: and dispositions, 16; indeterminacy of rational, 16, 176–79